SEPARATING GRAIN FROM CHAFF

RE-DEFINING LEADERSHIP ABOUT ITS TRUE MEANING

KAMIL TOUME

Copyright © 2020 Kamil Toume

ISBN: 9781710349450

All rights reserved, including the right to reproduce this book, or portions thereof in any form. No part of this text may be reproduced, transmitted, downloaded, decompiled, reverse engineered, or stored, in any form or introduced into any information storage and retrieval system, in any form or by any means, whether electronic or mechanical without the express written permission of the author.

This is a work of fiction. Names and characters are the product of the author's imagination and any resemblance to actual persons, living or dead, is entirely coincidental.

NOTE FROM THE AUTHOR

'This book is not written for the conformists, but rather for the leaders who are determined to use the purposeful and humane approaches of leadership to contribute to a vastly different, humane, and better world in the 21st century'.

CONTENTS

CONNECTING THE DOTS 7

WHAT A 100,000-YEAR JOURNEY TELLS US 19

    WHY DID SOME HUMAN SPECIES GO EXTINCT WHILE OTHERS SURVIVED TO BE US? 20

    WHAT MAKES US HUMANS? 23

DECODING THE PAST TELLS THE FUTURE 25

    HOW DID HUMANS START TO BUILD GREAT CULTURES? 26

    HOW DID GREAT CIVILIZATIONS FALL? 28

    WHY DID THE MAYA CIVILIZATION CEASE TO EXIST? 34

HISTORY CONTINUES TO REPEAT ITSELF IN THE BUSINESS WORLD 42

    HOW GREED SANK THE SHIP 43

    PUNCHING ABOVE ITS WEIGHT BLOWS UP IN ITS FACE 46

    THE BROTHERS DID NOT USE LOGIC AT ALL 49

UNDERSTANDING THE ROOTS OF THE PROBLEM CHANGES THE RESPONSE 53

    MONEY, GREED AND POWER JUSTIFY THE MEANS 60

    MANIPULATION HAS BECOME A PROFESSION IN THE AGE OF CONFUSION 65

THE SEEDS OF COLLAPSE HAVE BLOSSOMED 82

THE COLLAPSE IS IRREVERSIBLE 87

AN ACCIDENT IS NOT A COINCIDENCE; IT IS A SERIES OF INCIDENTS 89

TOWARDS A UNIVERSALLY ACCEPTED DEFINITION AND STANDARD FOR LEADERSHIP 93

REDEFINING ENTREPRENEURSHIP ABOUT ITS TRUE MEANING: .. 95

REDEFINING LEADERSHIP ABOUT ITS TRUE MEANING 147

THE POWER OF QUESTIONS IS POWERFUL 155

5 Ws AND AN H 156

LET US REDEFINE LEADERSHIP TO CREATE A BETTER WORLD ... 173

NOTES 177

ACKNOWLEDGEMENTS 182

ABOUT THE AUTHOR 183

CONNECTING THE DOTS

LANDING their first job after graduation is something that most people can never forget, and is at the forefront of memories when we get older and progress in our careers. I started my first job at a training company in September 2006 in Syria. The first four months were unforgettable. My excitement was up to the roof and my energy was palpable. I was profoundly motivated and dedicated to getting up every single day to go to work and learn new things, but all of that disappeared quickly. The company was going through some financial difficulties. Consequently, the board met to discuss a proposal for budget cuts to save money for the business. They opted for layoffs to balance the books.

On that day, I was having a normal conversation with my manager Safwan Sibai and two other colleagues. An hour later, I was on my way out when Mr. Sibai asked me to stay for a while. I looked at him and asked, "Is there a problem?" He just handed me a letter without saying anything. It was my termination notice. I finished reading the letter wondering why it happened like this despite my dedication and hard work. I took the letter and proceeded to leave. As I opened the door he said, "Do not be in a rush; I have something to tell you." To which I replied, ""Why? I lost my job, and nobody cares."

Mr. Sibai paused for a moment and gave me another letter titled 'resignation', and to my surprise, it was his resignation letter. I then suffered a third shock when I was handed another letter to read: an apology letter to Mr. Sibai about the decision to terminate my employment contract. As it turned out, Mr. Sibai opposed the termination decision and subsequently chose to resign as he could not accept it nor enforce it. His resignation came as a shock to the senior management, and as a result, they reconsidered their position. My position was not terminated after all. I asked myself why someone in his position would resign and lose his job for one of his staff members.

Mr. Sibai made the point clear the next day by telling me that leadership is not a position, it is an action. He explained, "To lead is to go first and face the danger for the people in your custody, not to sacrifice them for the perks of the position you hold." Mr. Sibai not only saved my job but also taught me a valuable lesson about leadership, which is that a leader is more of a responsibility than a position.

Over the next 13 years of working in different countries and industries in various administration and HR roles, I have observed and learned that management practices exercised by most managers have negatively affected people. Most managers and leaders are lost in mistaken business beliefs and practices inherited from the industrial and factory model of management. It is disgraceful that management thinking has not changed over the last 200 years. Unfortunately, replacing people to balance the numbers is still the prevalent management model.

...

In 2015, I was witness to an incident that happened with one of my colleagues who was the finance manager of the company for the previous five years. Drawing to the close of the financial year, the CEO decided to make some budget cuts to save some money and proposed layoffs to tackle the problem. Downsizing the company was the decision made by the CEO even though different solutions were presented to him by the finance manager to avoid the layoffs. A month later, the CEO made his decision and dismissed several employees, including the finance manager.

On his way back home that day, the finance manager fainted in the train station due to the stress that he had experienced all day in the office. By mere coincidence, there was a doctor nearby who was able to give him medicine and help him regain his strength to go home. The finance manager spent a week in the hospital suffering the results of the layoff. The CEO was steadfast in his decision and did not listen to the various solutions presented to him by all staff members to produce savings without resorting to the layoffs.

WHAT IS THE ROOT OF THIS THINKING?

Whom do we blame in this situation? Perhaps we should blame the managers or the educational systems that raised them to these standards? The best example of this argument comes from Alvin

Toffler who decried the 'Industrial Era School' in his 1970 book *Future Shock*:

> Mass education was the ingenious machine constructed by industrialism to produce the kind of adults it needed. The problem was inordinately complex. How to pre-adapt children for a new world—a world of repetitive indoor toil, smoke, noise, machines, crowded living conditions, collective discipline, a world in which time was to be regulated not by the cycle of sun and moon, but by the factory whistle and the clock. The solution was an educational system that, in its very structure, simulated this new world. This system did not emerge instantly. Even today it retains throw-back elements from pre-industrial society. Yet the whole idea of assembling masses of students (raw material) to be processed by teachers (workers) in a centrally located school (factory) was a stroke of industrial genius.

The current education system is set up to produce workers who comply and lack the courage to question practices or stand up for their principles. The result is leaders who speak proudly about corporate achievements but their actions rarely lead to significant changes in people's lives. The factories model of management has discouraged most leaders from making serious attempts to carry out significant transformations. One of the most common failures for leaders is that they are overtaken by a dictated mechanical and corporate style of management that only serves to demotivate and stress people.

The unwillingness to effect dramatic changes in the current capitalist system demonstrates that emphasis remains on the pace of production and the exponential growth of profits rather than people. The mission of corporatism is to keep the standing system, which is designed for compliance and obedience.

...

In February 2009, my mother was diagnosed with brain cancer. Her battle with this disease was uncomfortable. The doctors were talented sales professionals who convinced us to try all the options including chemotherapy, radiotherapy, and surgery. They exploited us emotionally to pay more to save my mother. They were experimenting on my mother for profit. Sadly, my mother suffered painfully and passed away in September 2009. In January 2017, I read a book titled *World Without Cancer: The Story of Vitamin B17* written by G. Edward Griffin. After reading this book and many other books addressing cancer and the available cures, I have become utterly convinced that the butchers, namely the doctors who were supposedly looking after my mother, had poisoned and slaughtered her. Reading, researching different sources and books, and remembering my mother suffering awoke me to the fact that the doctors and the hospitals were doing business not treating my mother.

Through common sense, reading, and Googling, it is clear that most cures are available in vegetables and different seeds and herbs. It is what we drink, eat, and consume that either boost or damage our health. Most of what we eat is nutritionally modified and unhealthy. Rarely did my grandparents hear about cancer, but today it is the constant subject of news headlines. I asked why, and I encourage you to question why cancer has become the most popular disease over the last 50 years.

Most doctors parrot information learned in medical schools, which are mostly funded by the pharmaceutical companies. Their business model would become obsolete if there was a shortage in the number of patients. These pharmaceutical corporations have deployed an army of sales reps, officially known as doctors, to promote their products. For those who will jump now and say that I am taking the conspiracy theorist view, I would encourage them to open their eyes and minds and use common sense to observe what is happening around them. Turning a blind eye, a deaf ear, a shut mouth, and a dead mind to what I read, learned, understood, heard, and witnessed does not suit me. I cannot close my eyes, bite my tongue, and parrot what they want us to parrot. Put up and shut up is not for me.

...

Had I continued my MBA, I would never have written this book and discovered my life purpose. If I had studied and learned what they wanted me to learn, I would never have found the truth away from all sorts of trickery and manipulation. When I started researching the content of this book, I was reading different kinds of books in history, anthropology, social economics, human psychology, and neurology, etc. By contemplating a quote from Winston Churchill, "The further you look into the past, the further you can see into the future," I was able to see the importance of connecting the dots to understand the full picture.

It became apparent to me that traditional education is primarily designed to develop rote skills and not the thinking muscle; it is about memorizing and learning but not yearning. Most of the taught concepts and theories are outdated, misleading, inaccurate, unsounded, and impractical. There is an overdose of information, without instruction on how to utilize it. As my book research progressed, I discovered why I vehemently hated the MBA program and struggled to ignite my passion. Traditional education teaches students to obey the rules, not to challenge them. I am not criticizing the MBA program that I dropped out for the sake of criticizing; I have my reasons that expedited my decision.

How do you trust an MBA program in which the marketing course teaches the 7-Ps—product, price, place, promotion, people, process, and physical evidence—but the most fundamental "P" is overlooked and disregarded? I am referring to the "purpose" of the business. The reason why the company exists impacts all its critical business functions, including marketing. If the company is purposeless, the products and offerings are purposeless too. The focus of the marketing courses is on highlighting the products' unique selling points and on competing based on lower prices and discounts. They forget to teach that good marketing is about communicating the value that the business is creating and how it is contributing, not the trivial differences

Also, they forget to teach that the power of good competition is learning, and the beauty of learning is continuous improvement. Most marketing courses fail to teach that leaders' sights should be focused on solving and achieving what they set to achieve rather than fixated on outsmarting and outpacing competitors.

How do you trust an MBA program in which the economics course requires an interpreter to understand the gibberish jargon? Confusion and ambiguity are critical in compiling economic courses because simplicity will lead to debunking the misconceptions, which is the most undesirable outcome. They teach us that debt can be paid off, but this is impossible in the current banking system. Central banks create a debt-based currency and lend to governments. To simplify, if the central bank creates a million dollars and charges 2% interest, how is this interest paid? Where does it come from? It does not exist at all. It must first be created by the central bank then borrowed.

How do you trust an economics course that teaches inflation as a continual and sustained increase in the price of goods and services? What a misleading definition! Inflation is an economic trickery performed by private corporations known as central banks that print money (aka 'fiat currency') out of thin air. When the prices of goods increase, it means the central banks have loaded the printing press with full ink cartridges at full capacity to print fiat currency and inject the market. Who is responsible for increasing prices continually and crunching parts of your monthly income? Understanding the definition changes the whole game.

How do you trust an MBA program in which people are deliberately dehumanized by referring to them as "resources" like raw materials, goods, and inventory? Most companies' HR practices are inherited from teachings that are still based on the mentality of the industrial age management in which people are replaceable and disposable in times of financial meltdowns and crises. Most business schools and organizations fail to understand that people do not desire to be managed or led; they want inspiration. Most performance management systems are still using "the rat race" that refers to the carrot-at-the-end-of-the-stick approach in reference to a cart driver dangling a carrot in front of a mule to get it to move forward.

Another issue is the hire and fire culture that recruits people at the speed of light and fires them at the stroke of a pen. The list goes on to include other courses that copy and paste the same formula that teaches students to conform and not to think, to pass the test individually and not to solve a problem collectively, and to seek a job and not to create one. How do you respect an educational system that has all these flaws that remain uncorrected and unchallenged?

Going through these experiences and other major life changes has made me pass the point of no return. It has challenged and mobilized me to pursue my new life quest. Even though I struggled to define my purpose and life mission in the beginning, after contemplating and thinking of what I have encountered, I was able to connect all the threads and see the full picture. I got to know myself in terms of what I stand for in the world and what I want to achieve. I discovered my life purpose: **"To challenge status quos, especially the most dehumanizing, to change the way we live our lives."**

I inherently know that countless confrontations are needed. A journey of a thousand miles begins with a single step and writing this book is the first step in putting my purpose into action to start this mission. My quest is not about fighting and revolting. I do not believe in revolutions; rather, I believe in inspiration. This book is about inspiring and embracing change to make things better.

. . .

"THE FARTHER BACK YOU CAN LOOK, THE FARTHER FORWARD YOU ARE LIKELY TO SEE."

— WINSTON CHURCHILL

CHAPTER ONE

WHAT A 100,000-YEAR JOURNEY

TELLS US

WHY DID SOME HUMAN SPECIES GO EXTINCT WHILE OTHERS SURVIVED TO BE US?

Around 70,000 years ago, *Homo sapiens*, the only surviving species of the genus *Homo* migrated from Africa to different places over the globe, developing mentally, physically, and culturally to the areas in which they settled. The culture they adopted allowed them to discover a new way of life using an accumulation of knowledge, indicating they had developed new capacities over their predecessors. A unique culture of survival unfolded. The culture of survival united *H. sapiens* in groups, as they were hunters and gatherers living in small populations that fostered their cooperation. The challenge of moving out of Africa presented them with many barriers that led them to develop new mental abilities.

These mental abilities enabled early humans to deal with the harsh weather in different places and to overcome the threat of food scarcity. Many scientific and anthropological findings indicate the disappearance of the Neanderthals, an extinct species who lived in northern Europe, coincided with the migration of *H. sapiens* and their arrival in Europe. Why did the Neanderthals vanish?

Many researchers have argued that *H. sapiens'* socialization has a significant correlation with the evolution of their brain size. These brain capacities are unique to anthropoid primates. It is scientifically proven that the Neanderthals were less sociable as they had smaller frontal brain regions, which are responsible for the cognitive abilities. The shorter the period of socialization, the longer the new cognitive abilities took to develop. Also, the size of the social network contributed to the development of cognitive competencies. This relation was first proposed in the 1990's by a British anthropologist, Robin Dunbar, who found a correlation between primate brain size and average social group size.

Dunbar suggested that humans can only comfortably maintain 150 stable relationships and this limit is a direct function of the relative neocortex size. Indeed, a combination of things led to the disappearance of the Neanderthals. The harsh and cold weather combined with a lack of knowledge to hunt compared with their new competitors, *H. sapiens,* proved fatal for the Neanderthals. Scattered groups whose methods of survival revealed great evidence of their inability to foster interaction and maintain cultural innovation. Thus, the cooperating *H. sapiens* mobilized their culture as a useful tool to gain the upper hand in the surviving game.

Neanderthals were physically stronger than the *H. sapiens.* They evolved as an adaptation to the dark and cold nights of Europe. It begs the question: Why did the weaker *H. sapiens* survive and populate the planet, whereas the stronger Neanderthals did not? Neanderthals minded their business in small groups; they did not cultivate a thriving culture, as their knowledge was limited to their smaller population. The lack of cognitive competencies limited the Neanderthals' ability to develop tools for hunting, which was critical for their survival, as well as their understanding to predict and manage the future. Consequently, they perished in the cold. *H. sapiens'* life was more than just about survival. Working and cooperating to survive served their higher pursuit, which was to explore and discover the new world. They found new ways to live and bond together to thrive as a group.

Forming strong social groups for hunting, gathering, eating, raising children, and defending each other against predators gave them a greater advantage not only to survive but also to thrive and keep moving. *H. sapiens* put themselves on the wheel of life. From hunting and gathering to farming, building cities and civilizations, to modern-day and our advanced way of living. Having a common goal and a shared destiny allowed them to cooperate and survive to discover the new world. They were cultural animals. That was their competitive advantage.

WHAT MAKES US HUMANS?

I grew up in a village in which watching and observing animals became a daily habit. I always wondered about the main difference between humans and other species regarding biological and cognitive makeup. What differentiates us from other species and animals? That central question boggled my mind. Embarking on the research to write this book enabled me to understand that humans developed complex social systems over an extended period, allowing them to improve cognitive abilities and manage several groupings. That would not have happened without interaction with each other, looking after each other, and protecting each other to survive and live another day.

The absence of a language limited cultural complexity. Without the vast exchange of information and knowledge among humans, their tools and way of life would have halted their survival. Language allowed humans to vastly exchange and share knowledge over generations to build the intellectual capacity that has become the hallmark of our species. Language did not evolve overnight; it was a series of experimentations instigated by human needs. It is the accumulation of the experience through the developed symbols and letters that we call writing and language. They transmitted human knowledge and set our cultural evolution, which no other animals ever had. Language has enabled humans to make an accelerating quantum leap over history.

Animals have their language like humans. Cows 'moo', horses 'neigh', dogs 'bark', and even ants know how to communicate in sophisticated ways that humans cannot understand or decipher. Parrots can say anything we say and imitate every word we pronounce. Birds communicate, but they do not have our sophisticated brains and languages that enabled us to build great cultures. History shows us that language and trade paved the way for the formation of societies, empires, and modern cities. Nothing could be organized in the same way if humans had not developed language ability. Language distinguishes humans from animals, and it is behind the ability to create ideas and innovations that fostered our survival. The interaction and learning among early humans over history led to the fundamental shift from hunting and gathering to agriculture.

CHAPTER TWO

DECODING THE PAST TELLS THE FUTURE

HOW DID HUMANS START TO BUILD GREAT CULTURES?

The agriculture revolution set humankind on the road to progress. Farming provided surplus that allowed humans to specialize in occupations other than agriculture. Hunting and gathering were no longer needed. Agriculture was the catalyst for the emergence of complex societies composed of groups of tribes. As the societies grew more complicated, the ruling class carried out all the decisions and maintained order. They were the early form of government and people depended on them to resolve their issues and disputes. The rulers were the few rich who assumed divine authority and were deputies of God on earth.

The top-down pyramid came into existence at that time. Food reserves enriched the few and enabled them to live in their ivory towers and become rulers and kings. The villagers worked and produced for the kings, and the kings protected the villagers from any conquest by the rival outsiders. The development of cities preceded the rise of civilizations. The last 4,000 years witnessed the birth of civilizations that stood great for centuries.

Most civilizations had common systems that characterized them, including the hierarchical social order, a centralized system for distributing wealth, cultural and religious traditions, languages, etc. Trade paved the way for essential resources and was the catalyst to the development and expansion of all civilizations throughout history. The Roman Empire controlled much of the land from England to Mesopotamia. A series of stages from their peak times traveling along the declining trajectory of history before collapsing at the end has become a repeated pattern. With the successions of civilizations, history has started the process of repeating itself.

HOW DID GREAT CIVILIZATIONS FALL?

THE COLLAPSE OF THE ROMAN EMPIRE

The boundaries of the Roman Empire extended in all directions from England to Spain across Europe along the northern coast of Africa to Egypt and central Asia. Geography shaped the rise of the Roman civilization. The Tiber River was the Romans competitive advantage over their rivals as it allowed them to secure a source of water and gain access to the rest of the Mediterranean Sea. The geographical position put them far enough away to escape the pirates' raids from the sea.

At the time it became a republic, Rome was still a small city surrounded by enemies. Romans were strong soldiers, the discipline in the army was harsh, and the deserters faced death penalties. This strict discipline turned the Roman soldiers into gladiators who did not give up easily. As Romans expanded through Italy, they built permanent military settlements in the areas they conquered, and then they built roads to link these towns. These roads facilitated the movement of troops to any place in their growing territory. To rule and control, the Romans created a system in which Romans gave full citizenship to selected people, especially Italians. These citizens could vote, serve in the government, and were treated equally to other citizens under the law.

The concept of social comparison profoundly influenced the distinction between the ruling and the working classes. The government positions did not go to the working class despite their tax payments that helped the republic to thrive. Striving to get equal rights with the ruling class led the working class to rebel in 494 BC. The workers and the villagers refused to serve in the army and set up a republic of their own.

Things started to deteriorate in 107 BC when Gaius Marius, one of the military leaders, changed the military recruitment strategy. He recruited non-Roman soldiers who were paid to join the Roman army. The paid soldiers did not give their loyalty to the Roman Empire, but rather they were loyal to the money paid to them by the military commanders. The paid soldiers were fighting for money, and they were unwilling to risk their lives and die. The sense of patriotism for the Romans deteriorated massively, and they became indifferent to the destiny of their empire.

The rulers of the vast empire, with borders extending from Britain to North Africa to Asia, had no idea how to deal with the large size and the growing problems of the empire. The vast geographical size increased military logistical and administrative costs. The factors that led to the fall of the Roman Empire were many, but the unjustified expansion that increased its geographical size topped the list.

- **UNJUSTIFIED EXPANSION:** The vast increase in the geographical size of the empire caused a problem in the necessity to defend its borders and territories. Barbarians who hated the Romans inhabited most of the conquered lands.

- **FRACTURED ECONOMY:** Had the Romans kept the amounts of gold and silver in the minted coins unchanged, they would not have been able to increase spending and wage more wars. They were faced with the issue of how to fund a war and pay for the soldiers' salaries with a limited supply of gold and silver. Solving this challenge made the Romans the source of inspiration for most governments and central banks today. The solution proposed by the Romans was to debase the coins in circulations.

The purity of the Roman coinage decreased massively, and less purity meant more silver coins resulting in more spending and waging more wars. More coins of poor quality channeled wealth away from the ordinary Romans. Also, the scarcity of the precious metals left the government with no options but to increase taxes on the Romans to sustain the empire. Hyperinflation infiltrated the empire and led to its collapse. What started with the Romans continued to cause most of the wars and financial crises, and it is one of the most ever ignored problems of our time.

- **MILITARY:** In the army, the loyalty of the soldiers was not to the empire and its ideals; it was to the commanders who fought for their selfish interests. The government began to recruit mercenaries: foreign soldiers who were fighting for money and not for the destiny of the empire. The sense of pride and loyalty for the average Roman citizens weakened to such a degree that the Romans who had previously sacrificed their lives for the republic became later indifferent to its fate. When the Germanics attacked Rome and stole its treasures, the Roman army did not defend their city. In fact, they questioned why they should risk their lives to support a corrupt and decaying society.

Some people say that Rome fell because of the Germanic tribes' attack. It is contrary to the fact that the Romans lost their sense of belonging to their empire, which was no longer upholding the greater glory of the past. Rome killed itself as it diminished its status and made its citizens indifferent to its fate. History repeats itself, and this is what people fail to understand.

...

History repeats itself, and this is what people fail to understand.

WHY DID THE MAYA CIVILIZATION CEASE TO EXIST?

In Mesoamerica in 900 CE, the Mayans were paving the way to becoming one of the mightiest empires when suddenly their civilization collapsed. What happened? Was it their political, military, or religious system? The matter of fact is that it was all of them. The Mayan Empire consisted of competing states, and their ideology was heavily dependent on religious manifestations. The shapes and the architecture of the buildings bear witness to that. The kings and priests inhabited the large buildings, and the ordinary people built the cities and the temples.

In his book, *Collapse, How Societies Choose to Fail or Succeed*, Professor Jared Diamond provided a framework for understating the disintegration and the fall of the Maya civilization. Some of the factors that contributed to the Mayan demise included a damaging environment, fierce competition, hostilities among the kings, waging wars, and building huge monuments rather than solving their problems.

The Mayan cities hosted vast populations ruled by the elites who possessed divine authorities. The massive temples were constructed toward the sky, the sun, and the moon to celebrate and glorify the accomplishments of their godly leaders. The dot-com of today was the competition among the Mayan rulers to construct bigger temples and buildings. Competition was very aggressive and led to the eruption of most of the Mayan Wars. The wars overtaxed the people and put constant pressure on them. Overpopulation and limited natural resources intensified competition among the Mayans, which aggravated the rules of the natural selection game.

The Mayans fought and competed for fewer resources because of their conflicts and the wars that ensued. The self-enrichment through waging wars, extracting more from the people to support their activities, and ignoring the problems that cracked their societies were seemingly the reasons that undermined the Maya civilization. One of the intellectual problems of all social sciences has long been why civilizations follow a trajectory that in general fails to stabilize. Professor Diamond has contemplated this question in terms of what it tells us about the very nature of societies. Indeed, how a society disintegrates tells us much about how it was structured in the first place.

SOME NATIONS HAVE BEEN ENGINEERED TO FAIL THEN FALL

THE COLLAPSE OF THE SOVIET UNION

The Soviet Union was born in 1917. The Marxist revolutionary Vladimir Lenin was the first Soviet leader and the leader of the Bolshevik Revolution. Lenin's regime was oppressive, and he demanded the allegiance of every Russian citizen. Under the rule of Joseph Stalin in 1924, the totalitarian regime took over all the functions of the state. State leaders were not permitted to voice opinions or to argue against Stalin's laws. People who did were sent off to death camps or tortured. The vision of the Soviet Union was a military one. They poured all their capital into military production, and it was the ultimate example of economic unproductivity. Their war machines and weapons were very advanced, whereas their computers and technological devices lagged behind those in the West.

Corruption and bureaucracy were the hallmarks of the Soviet system. Innovation and prosperity were impossible in a country where the destructive arms race paved the way to its collapse. Mikhail Gorbachev, President of the Soviet Union (1990–1991) decided to unleash the enterprise spirit in the Soviet economy. He loosened the government's grip on the business sector. He believed that private initiative would lead to innovation. With this decision, individuals could own businesses for the first time since the 1920's.

The Soviet Union was admitted metaphorically to the Intensive Care Unit in 1980. The nation's savior, Mikhail Gorbachev, strived hard to correct the nosedive of his country, but his mission had failed before it started. Gorbachev planted the seeds of innovation and prosperity, but good seeds need good soil to grow. The old totalitarian system failed the new system. Granting more freedom to citizens, participating in elections, and allowing the publications of newspapers and books were some of the introduced policies. However, these new policies could not resurrect the Soviet Union. In his farewell speech, Gorbachev summed up the problem, "The old system collapsed before the new one had time to begin working."

On December 25, 1991, the Soviet Union officially ended when Gorbachev conceded power after demonstrations went viral across the nation. The Soviet Union did not fall overnight; the seeds of destruction were sown early. The outcome was the emergence of newly formed independent countries. Self-regulating economies and political systems were the daunting tasks of the newly emerging nations under very divisive and bitter territorial and political disputes. The collapse was unstoppable.

NORTH KOREA

In North Korea, the state owns everything and it confiscates and controls everything related to its people. People in North Korea struggle to manage their own lives. The government's grip on the political, economic, social, and technological aspects has made North Koreans struggle to survive and prosper. The leadership of Kim Jong-Il turned the country into a monopolistic, isolated, and oppressed island that denies people's rights. 'We own everything and give little in return' is the economic policy in North Korea. Enjoying economic prosperity for the North Koreans constitutes a grave violation of Kim Jong-Il's rule. People are only allowed to work to pay for their basics.

The technological revolution at the turn of the 20th century around the world did not benefit the North Koreans, as they do not have access to non-state radio or TV channels. Even watching an authorized media is a punishable crime. People's phone calls are monitored, censored, and intercepted. Possessing a USB or DVD containing Western films is a felony. Telephoning someone overseas makes any North Korean subject to government tracking and interrogation. In their book, *Why Nations Fail*, Daron Acemoglu and James A. Robinson explained why North Koreans live under such poor economic conditions and lag behind most of their counterparts in the developed countries. The simple answer is that is impossible to build an inclusive economic institution on an extractive political system. In other words, if the political system of any country is corrupt, dictatorial, and unreformed, the possibility of creating a prosperous economic system is doomed.

On the other side of the Korean Island, the South Korean government gave their people all sorts of incentives to unleash their potential and entrepreneurial spirit. The sound political system propelled the economic system to make a quantum leap forward driving productivity and enriching the South Koreans. The North Korean political system massively failed to reform its country, which puts the people's will in a constant struggle with Kim Jong hardliners. The result is a failed state.

COLLAPSE IS NOT BY DEFAULT; IT IS HUMAN-MADE

History speaks volumes about the collapse of civilizations. The last 12,000 years witnessed the rise and fall of small, medium, and large empires. Hundreds of books have been written on the subject. History scholars, archaeologists, and anthropologists have presented irrefutable proofs about the factors that contributed to the rise as well as the demise of civilizations. The behavior of the elites originated from a materialistic basis as opposed to a moral one. Few favored the interests of the community over their short-term interests. Extracting more wealth and exercising greater power governed their behavior. Consequently, all of them were destined to fail and fall. Collapse does not fall from the sky, and the sky does not rain failure seeds on earthly kingdoms.

The rulers throughout history and in our modern times sowed the seeds of their collapse. It is about destroying the people's sense of pride and discouraging their genuine contribution to their nations. All of that was to extract more and give back less. No matter how small or large the empires and states were, they were built to enrich the elites. Eventually, all were destined to develop cracks that caused the downfall of the entire system. This led inevitably to catastrophic suffering and outcomes not only for the people but also for the elites themselves. It is not my assumption; It is history, "Collapse is not by default; it is always human-made."

CHAPTER THREE

HISTORY CONTINUES TO REPEAT ITSELF IN THE BUSINESS WORLD

Many of the greatest civilizations, such as the Romans, the Mayans, the Sumerians, the Akkadians, the Persians, the Chinese, and many others, became great tales in history books. Superpowers declined and collapsed, the sun set on the British Empire, and the Soviet Union ceased to exist. Have we learned from the lessons of the past? The answer is no. Most people have the opportunity to visit museums to see remnants of the past and study history to decode and explore the future, but few have discovered the truth. History continues to repeat itself; the cycle is unstoppable and continues to provide us with examples that are relevant to the business world.

HOW GREED SANK THE SHIP

The merger between Houston Natural Gas and InterNorth, a Nebraska pipeline company, gave birth to Enron, an American energy company based in Houston, Texas. The merger led Enron to accrue a massive debt, after which they were unable to generate enough cash to stay in business. The deteriorating situation put pressure on Enron to come up with an innovative financial strategy to float itself and make profits. Kenneth Lay, the CEO of Enron appointed Jeffery Skilling who saved Enron from the fall. Skilling invented the tools that allowed Enron to control the energy industry and turn natural gas into a trading commodity. Skilling's intelligence led Enron to dominate the market for natural gas contracts, help it to foretell the future prices, and make astronomical profits.

Enron's corporate culture reflected Skilling's character and his aggressive strategy to control and seize the whole market. Moreover, to match the plan, Enron sought to hire the best traders who could earn maximum profits and outpace its biggest rivals. The law of the jungle was the law inside Enron that permitted traders to eat what they hunted. Skilling hired 29-year-old Andrew Fastow, as the new game required a financial gladiator. Fastow's progression on the career ladder to be the CFO was peerless. The common greedy interests between the strategic architect and the financial one were strikingly unrestrained.

The culture inside Enron forced traders to do whatever it took to generate more profits in a competitive environment. They became more target driven and obsessed with hitting profit targets, which ensured the longevity of their jobs in the company. Skilling's most exceptional invention was the creation of the performance review committee, which ranked and yanked people on a very harsh scale. The higher the traders earned profits, the longer they stayed in the company. Layoffs always received Skilling's full endorsement, and he was very famous for dismissing 20% of the workforce every year. Internal competition and the race among traders to post high earnings were prized and valued more than the employees' overall potential and growth. However, Enron's foundations were developing cracks, and the house of cards had begun to crumble.

The crony accounting standard 'Mark to market accounting' allowed Enron to record potential profits on specific projects immediately after contracts were signed, regardless of the actual earnings that the deals would generate. This gave Enron the chance to look profitable even when it was not. Enron's financial statements were confusing and unanalyzable to the investors, shareholders, and analysts.

Misleading financial statements, sophisticated business models, and data mismanagement were used to misrepresent the phony earnings and false financial performance. The greed of Wall Street investment banks facilitated Fastow's job, the bright CFO. Enron's stock price was the North Star, and most of the deals were leveraged with the stock. Further, the accounting firm Arthur Andersen acted as a partner rather than an auditor, as the company shared a piece of the pie with Enron.

In February 2001, Lay retired and named Skilling the new president and CEO of Enron. Skilling himself resigned, citing "personal reasons." Lay largely ignored many warnings that the company was heading toward a financial disaster. He repeatedly assured employees as well as the public that Skilling left for personal reasons and that the company was financially stable. At the same time, the board fired Andy Fastow, the CFO after discovering that he had embezzled more than $30 million from Enron through his companies. On December 2, 2001, Enron filed for one of the largest bankruptcies in U.S. history. Most employees lost their pensions and investors lost over $11 billion in shareholder value.

PUNCHING ABOVE ITS WEIGHT BLOWS UP IN ITS FACE

In 1995, Swissair entered a dark tunnel when they started buying bankrupt airlines all over Europe. A unique strategy developed by McKinsey consultancy, called the 'hunter strategy' made Swissair easy prey for other competitors. On Oct 2, 2001, Swissair made the news headlines; they grounded all flights due to a cash crisis. Most Swissair passengers were unable to reach their destinations. Their tickets were worthless, as other airlines did not recognize them. In some airports, passengers who waited for long hours had to sleep on airport floors.

The deregulation of the aviation industry in 1978 in the United States exposed most airlines worldwide to fierce competition. Increasing profit margins made most companies lower their services and standards. New cheap operators such as Ryanair, EasyJet, and Buzz shared the pie. The problem for Swissair was that they wanted to be a global player, but they were too small," claimed Sepp Moser, an aviation analyst. Becoming a global player led them to establish hubs where airlines had to link their intercontinental flights to achieve a higher number of passengers. It was the hallmark of the surviving strategy in the aviation industry.

McKinsey's hunter strategy for Swissair allowed them to become hunters, but they did not understand global business. Soon, Swissair expanded to become the 4th largest European airline. Swissair acquired shares in the French AOM, Belgium's Sabena, and the Portuguese TAP. However, the international competition had sliced part of their profits, as most of them, including Swissair, were struggling financially.

While Swissair was acquiring shares in financially struggling companies, London Heathrow, Paris Charles de Gaulle, and Amsterdam forged and developed international alliances. Although portfolio diversification is necessary, focus is critical. Swissair's portfolio was diversified and included non-aviation activities in hoteling, aircraft leasing, maintenance, and duty-free shops to name a few. Those activities accounted for more than of Swissair group.

Following 9/11 in America, the number of airline passengers fell, and credit lines were tightened to finance ambitious investment plans like those of Swissair. At that time, Swissair was sitting on a mountain of debt. Negotiations with the leading banks limited the acquisitions of smaller European airliners. Banks were reluctant and no longer prepared to inject more cash into Swissair without the management undertaking further cuts because Swissair had already drowned in debt. Like most of the CEOs and executives, Mario Corti, the chair of Swissair, resorted to layoffs to account for the loss. He dismissed 1,300 employees to stop the debt spiral.

The reasons that led to the demise of Swissair were many, but the history recursive pattern is easily recognizable. Swissair wanted to be a global player competing with British Airways, Air France, and

Lufthansa, but they were too small. Although banks' conspiracies, mismanagement inside Swissair, and the deregulation of the aviation industry were contributing factors, they did not cause the bankruptcy. The collapse was caused by the unjustified expansion strategy that brought Swissair to its knees. Ultimately, Swissair tried to hunt opportunities before other airlines, but they ended up being hunted themselves.

THE BROTHERS DID NOT USE LOGIC AT ALL

According to Wikipedia, in 2000, Alan Greenspan, **chair of the Federal Reserve of the United States,** raised interest rates several times; these actions were believed by many to have caused the bursting of the dot-com bubble. According to Nobel laureate Paul Krugman, however, "he didn't raise interest rates to curb the market's enthusiasm; he didn't even seek to impose margin requirements on stock market investors. Instead, he waited until the bubble burst, as it did in 2000, then tried to clean up the mess afterward." In autumn 2001, as a reaction to the September 11 attacks and various corporate scandals which undermined the economy, the Greenspan-led Federal Reserve initiated a series of interest cuts that brought down the Federal Funds rate to 1% in 2004."

In 2008, bailouts became the master scene in the financial rescue show, which was orchestrated by the chair of the Federal Reserve, Ben Bernanke, and the treasury secretary, Hank Paulson. Following 9/11, **the Federal Reserve lowered** interest rates, and banks started pouring money into borrowers' accounts extensively. **People accumulated more debt, as everyone wanted to own their dream house. Ripping massive profits out of the eased credits, the 4th largest of Wall Street investment banks, Lehman Brothers,** saw a big opportunity: some calculations showed that the bank would end up with astronomical profits if they invested in the real estate market.

Their prediction was right. Lehman Brothers began the process of acquiring mortgage lenders and became the master of securitized mortgages by pooling financial assets and turning them into tradable interest-bearing securities. Richard Fuld's, the chair of Lehman Brothers, strong appetite for the enormous profits from the securitized mortgages was unprecedented. Mr. Fuld's brutality and intimidation governed the culture of the bank. They borrowed excessively and invested massively in the mortgages market. Greed, selfishness, recklessness, and power led Lehman Brothers to put all their eggs in one basket.

The aggressive strategy of expansion in real estate made the bank highly vulnerable to the downfall in the housing prices. The irony of the Lehman Brothers firm lies in the fact that they had an army of risk management teams at every level, yet they fell into the trap of the market. Their failure was not a result of their assumptions and miscalculations with regards to the leverage ratios and the magnified losses, but it was their selfish greed, which blinded them to see the real risks in their mathematical models.

WHAT LED TO THE COLLAPSE OF LEHMAN BROTHERS?

Lehman Brothers' collapse was multidimensional. Below is a simple analysis of what contributed to the failure of Lehman Brothers and the financial crisis in 2008.

- Between 2001 and 2004, Alan Greenspan, the chair of the Federal Reserve lowered the interest rates to reach almost zero.
- During his presidency from 2000 until 2008, President George W. Bush vowed to spread the dream of homeownership. He signed the American Dream Down Payment Act of 2003 enabling Americans to overcome the hurdle of requiring a down payment to own a home.
- From 2003–2007, Fannie Mae and Freddie Mac, Merrill Lynch, Lehman Brothers, and other investment banks started creating collateralized debt obligations, most of which were toxic.
- In 2007, the Federal Reserve pushed the panic button by raising interest rates and causing a financial seizure. Ben Bernanke's reaction to the housing bubble was inaction.
- People could not afford to pay interest on the mortgages. Foreclosures started, and the banks began repossessing homes and stealing the real wealth of people.
- The Treasury and the Federal Reserve allowed some banks to go bankrupt, like Lehman Brothers, and saved others to seize up the system. Sinking some boats and saving others was the Federal Reserve's strategy to manage the financial crisis they created. Lehman Brothers was moving in the orbit of a highly gravitational greedy power. This power is the Federal Reserve, the eye of the storm that caused the financial crisis and its dire consequences.

As we will see in Chapter Four, Lehman's CEO was obsessed with making more money. Similar to the behavior of any addict, engaging in reckless and unaccountable activities is very popular and overcoming the habit is so difficult. His failure in saving the bank was not contributed only to his miscalculation and overconfidence in the bank, but also ascribed to his insatiable greed for money. He became addicted, and this inhibited the critical functional areas of his brain that would enable him to make sound decisions.

As Larry McDonald, a former Lehman vice-president, highlights in his book, *Colossal Failure of Common Sense*, Lehman's management team had no enterprise risk management system, no concept of risk management, no common language to address risk, nor any desire to listen to or to learn from risk-related concerns raised by anyone. "Now, we fully understand why Richard Fuld, the CEO of Lehman Brothers failed to realize the severity of the risk that his bank has undertaken. Lehman Brothers bank was the direct result of the reckless and imbalanced economic policies of the Federal Reserve that not only pushed the bank to the edge but to collapse into pieces on the 15th of Sept 2008."

CHAPTER FOUR

UNDERSTANDING THE ROOTS OF THE PROBLEM CHANGES THE RESPONSE

We assume that watching TV is a bad habit, but I discovered that it is a useful one when I started watching National Geographic documentaries, especially about plane crashes. In all the series that I watched, the commentary went like this, "Flying is one of the most comfortable and safest forms of transport, but what happens when tragedy strikes? What is likely to be the main cause of a passenger plane crashing? A faulty engineering design, mechanical failure, or pilots' mistakes?" Following any plane crash, investigators immediately identify many factors that could cause the accident, including engine failure, structural failures, adverse weather conditions, and even a possible bomb on the plane. Potential crew errors and negligence usually top the investigation list after the crash.

For example, on December 29, 1972, Eastern Airlines flight 401, flying from John F. Kennedy International Airport to Miami International Airport in the United States, crashed in Florida killing 101 people and causing 75 injuries. The crash happened because the crew was so preoccupied with a landing gear light. While checking the landing gear light, the pilot assistant accidentally switched off the autopilot causing the aircraft to lose control and descend. The crew realized too late that they were heading for a disaster. The plane lost altitude and crashed. Although loss of life is tragic, every single accident that is successfully investigated provides data that can be used to improve technology in the future.

Ludwig von Mises, a renowned Austrian economist, said, "Government is the only institution that can take a valuable commodity like paper and make it worthless by applying ink." Mises described inflation as a process by which the government increases the supply of money. The more plentiful the supply of money is, the higher the prices of goods. Businesses do not contribute to inflation; they respond to it. The distinction here makes a considerable difference. Who oversees the money supply? In other words, who is printing the money? Central banks not governments print money and lend to governments. Rising prices is a central bank business.

Understanding the roots of the problem changes the response not only for plane crashes and inflation-related problems but also for companies' failures as well. When companies face a risky situation, the normal business practice is that senior managers end up with a graph that nobody understands. The resulting data is compiled from a mixture of complicated analyses that do not diagnose the problem or provide a way to a solution. Such analyses usually further complicate the situation. Who is the main contributor to the fall and demise of companies? Are they the employees, the customers, the market conditions, the competition, or the management?

Like in plane crashes, external factors play an essential role in the nosedive, but they are not the primary reasons causing the plane to crash. Windy air, a storm, snow, and turbulence are contributing factors, but they are constants in the formula. The critical ones are the conditions inside the plane that determine its movement.

It is the same for buildings; great buildings are the ones that never shake to collapse. They are built on two foundations that support them and contribute to their strength and sustainability. These foundations are concrete and steel, both of which play an essential role in sustaining the durability and the strength of the building. It is the foundation and not the height of the building that matters. Greatness is measured by the strength of the foundations that will sustain the longevity of the building. Have you ever wondered why skyscrapers do not fall over? Why do bridges not sink into the rivers? The stability of a structure is measured by the degree to which it can hold weight and withstand forces that are placed on it.

By examining the impact of historical events in many ancient civilizations, countries, and companies, I have discovered a pattern that links all of them together. This pattern has contributed to their decline and collapse. However, their crash was not sudden and unexpected; the seeds of destruction were sown deeply within their structures from the beginning. It is not an overnight process as most people think when they consider what happened with Enron, Lehman Brothers, and other money-centric organizations.

The cracks were formed early from the time of laying the first foundation, and it was this first foundation that caused the disaster. Great buildings do not fall by themselves. When you ask civil engineers about what leads to the collapse of a building, they always point at the foundation upon which it was built. The more the foundation is reinforced, the stronger it endures external and internal pressures and tensions.

There are many reasons for the fall of civilizations, nations, and companies. Whom are we going to blame? Kings, governments, systems, geography, or history? Historians offer varying lists of criteria for the fall of civilizations, but most of the lists include the following important factors: a large population, food scarcity, a centralized government, controlling religion, and a hardworking and overtaxed population. It is impossible to point out a single factor, as there is a combination of many.

I have attempted to represent the various factors in an inverted pyramid. The reason the pyramid is inverted is to highlight the foundation as the main contributor to a collapse. This inverted paradigm summarizes the factors, causes, and symptoms that, when multiplied, form the trajectory of the downfall.

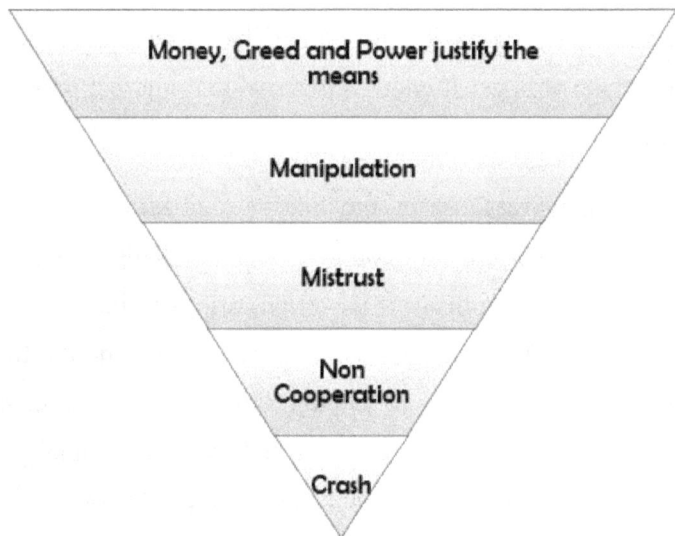

Figure 1: The Collapse Pyramid

WHAT IS THE PROBLEM?

Drawing to the end of the Ice Age 14,000 ago, a remarkable development occurred, temperatures increased and humans discovered a new way of life. They found an easier way to gather food and were able to live in smaller groups in the same place all year. Agriculture was the catalyst that enabled humans to farm, produce food, harvest, preserve, and have a surplus. Hunting and gathering disappeared.

By 10,000 BC, humans made a quantum leap by building their first settlements. They domesticated animals and cultivated wheat and barley, which fed larger groups of people. The food surplus led to the emergence of trade and exchange. It also led to the rise of a new class: the merchants. These people became enormously wealthy and powerful. Inequality arrived dividing humans into two groups: the rich and the poor.

This transformation was best described by Jerome Lewis, who was trained in anthropology at the London School of Economics:

> In these societies, the pressure is not put on people to produce, but on them to share whatever they have produced. When humans started to accumulate goods and had abundant resources, control over the distribution of vital resources promoted political inequality and hierarchy through the emergence of the elites, kings, and emperors. Their interest was to benefit themselves in short-term and ignore the long terms for their communities. These hierarchies, as history tells us, were organized with inequalities between peers, seniors, juniors, and gender groups. They were politically, socially, and economically unequal.

At this point in history, the ruling class did whatever suited their interests regardless of the means and the ways they used to achieve them. Since money, greed and power were the ends, all the means were justifiable. Today, history has repeated itself and time has taught us nothing. Can we turn the clock back? No, but we can learn from the past to put the lessons learned into actions to design and shape the future.

MONEY, GREED AND POWER JUSTIFY THE MEANS

As noted earlier, agriculture was the turning point in the human history, as it enabled humans to have a surplus of food for the first time. Taking a short glimpse throughout history, we discover how humans made the radical shift from a sharing community to an accumulating one. This journey is also about learning how money, greed and power were the dominant forces in shaping human behavior from 7,000 years ago until present day.

- **10,000 BC/HUNTERS AND GATHERERS:** Groups of people walked long distances, and hunted and gathered wild animals. They lived and socialized in smaller groups. The weather was harsh, nature was hard, and starvation was always just one step away. Hunting and gathering were the dominant tasks of their day, and they shared food to live and survive for the next day.

- **8,000 BC/FARMING:** The move from a hunter-gatherer lifestyle to a farming lifestyle made the transformational shift between a sharing community and an accumulating one. It was the turning point in human history, but it did not take place overnight. Early humans produced more food than they needed, and food surplus led to the birth of early forms of trade. The farmers became merchants, and the merchants became wealthy. The wealthy became rulers who ruled and exercised enormous power over people. The change that had taken place over time was vast and its impact played a significant role in the formation of our modern cities and societies.

- **4500 BC-1900 BC/SUMERIANS IN MESOPOTAMIA:** Trade was the backbone of the Sumerian economy. Recording trades, keeping accounts, controlling debt, and monitoring taxes led the Sumerians to discover writing. The wealthy were kings who controlled trade, and to preserve their kingship, they used the nation's wealth to wage more wars and drain more from society. The economic power turned into a top-down rule that took more and gave back less. The Sumerian civilization moved from prosperity to collapse.

- **753 BC–476 AD/THE ROMAN EMPIRE:** The Roman Empire was one of the greatest civilizations in the world, yet its structural decline took a steep nosedive before crashing. The Roman economy and tax structures overburdened the ordinary Romans. The Roman emperors debased the gold and silver coins in circulations to afford to pay for more wars. Paying the soldiers' salaries increased the spending tenfold. Hyperinflation infiltrated and disintegrated the empire. The wars brought the empire to its knees. The Romans distrusted their empire and emperors, and they felt indifferent to a rotten system that ruined their future.

- **9TH–17TH CENTURY/FEUDALISM & BOURGEOISIE IN EUROPE:** Feudalism was another way of concentrating power in the hands of the few. The few owned the lands and oppressed peasants and workers to produce and provide for them. The church played a more significant role in shaping feudalism. The concentration of power in the hands of a few was a very disruptive force. The system broke down gradually.

- Karl Marx (1818–1883) was a revolutionary German economist and philosopher and the founder of the Communist movement. Marx argued that the capitalist bourgeoisie exploited the proletariat, the working class. In his view, the work carried out by the proletariat created enormous wealth for the capitalist bourgeoisie. It was another form of social order through the exploitation of urban and rural workers.

- **17TH & 18TH CENTURIES/THE INDUSTRIAL REVOLUTION IN GREAT BRITAIN:** The industrial revolution began in Great Britain and spread to Europe and the United States. While industrialization brought about a variety of manufactured goods and a good lifestyle for the few, the majority suffered from poor working conditions and living standards. Long working hours, cruel discipline, and low wages were the outcomes of the industrialization.

- **21ST CENTURY/CORPORATE CAPITALISM:** Creating more wealth and concentrating it in the hands of one man is the doctrine of capitalism. Adam Smith, the father of capitalist theory and modern economics, proposed in his book *The Wealth of Nations* in 1776 a different capitalism that could work for the common good if the market was left to regulate itself without government interference. The concept of sound capitalism envisioned by Smith was practically unsound. It did not convey the real sense of the proposed capitalism. Making profits by tempting people to buy things they do not need is the main headline of today's capitalism.

- **AT PRESENT, THE INSATIABLE GREED FOR PROFITS DEHUMANIZED MOST BUSINESSES:** In today's business world, people have been lost sight of as human beings in a money chase pursuit in which maximizing profits has become the prime business motive. It has turned people into tradable commodities that are bought and sold in the marketplace. Greed, selfishness, and competitiveness prevail. Laying people off is done instantaneously at the stroke of a CEO pen without any hesitation.

Money, greed and power have been the dominant factors in shaping human behavior throughout history. To preserve them, emperors, kings, feudalists, bourgeoisie, business owners, CEOs, executives, and managers have exerted their power and influence to sway their people to enrich themselves at the expense of the whole society. However, this process has not succeeded in building momentum. Rather, this kind of manipulation has enslaved humanity throughout most of its history and still presents the most dangerous threat to our human race.

MANIPULATION HAS BECOME A PROFESSION IN THE AGE OF CONFUSION

Calling all Christians in Europe to fight Muslims to restore the Holy Land in the East was the speech delivered by Pope Urban II in November 1095. His words gave rise to the crusades' wars that made Christians descend in vast numbers on the birthplace of their religion. Taking back Jerusalem reinforced the power of the papacy in calling Christians to service the righteous war in the East by promising forgiveness of sins for all who died in the name of the Christ. However, helping fellow Christians was not the only motive that mobilized Christians to march on Jerusalem; they were also tempted by lands and treasures to be gained from the conquest.

The idea of manipulating public opinion is an ancient tool for political and religious consumption. Most kings and leaders throughout history created statues to promote their divine authority as representatives of God on earth. Naram Sin declared his divine power as an agent of God establishing his rule over the Akkad Empire. Naram was the husband of Ishtar, the goddess of war and love. Akkadians had to obey and serve them. Throughout history, herding the masses required the rulers to show their connection with God and how they fulfill his message on earth. Manipulation was the norm.

The following quote from Edward L. Bernays' book *Propaganda* describes how to organize mass chaos and how elites use propaganda to start wars and influence business, politics, and every aspect of our lives.

> We are governed, our minds are molded, our tastes formed, our ideas suggested, largely by men we have never heard of. This is a logical result of the way in which our democratic society is organized. In almost every act of our daily lives, whether in the sphere of politics or business, in our social conduct or our ethical thinking, we are dominated by the relatively small number of people who understand the mental processes and social patterns of the masses. It is they who pull the wires which control the public mind.

Today, companies around the world are highly engaged in studying, majoring in the ways and means of changing and binding minds to their convictions." Some are doing this for the common good, but the majority has selfish interests. Companies have marketing or public relation departments that are set up primarily for that purpose. Most companies nowadays are practicing manipulation on a daily basis. "Shopping around for salvation: The new religion is consumerism, and massive malls are its cathedrals. Let us bow our heads and pay" was an article published on November 3, 1993 in *The Independent* newspaper in the UK. This statement explains a lot about how capitalism and consumerism are manipulating us every day into seducing our desires to buy things that we do not inherently need. It is a matter of firing off neurons in our brains to be addicted and follow this religion that forces us to demand more with devotion and energy. Consumerism is the system under which we all live. Unfortunately, it fails miserably to meet the genuine needs of people, as profit comes before people and the environment.

Lower wages, longer hours, no job security, tedious jobs, and unnecessary products and services are the master scene of the business landscape today. Making a profit is the number one goal and perhaps the business' unquestionable purpose. Many companies have gone beyond the objective of making money; they have caused environmental and social disasters. They acted irresponsibly. Manipulation has become such a profession that I cannot tell the degree to which companies use it. Some call it public relations, marketing, or communication. Even though most companies are adorned with traditional and digital marketing, most of their communication is still manipulative and transactional.

Listening to marketing and communication managers, you will find all kinds of trickery and linguistic programming. They do not identify and come to grips with the fundamental problems that their communication is aimed at making people spend more today and excessively tomorrow. The new religion of consumerism used by corporations and businesses has manipulated people to work with the fear of losing jobs and taking pay cuts. It has also seduced consumers to bow their heads and pay more.

MANIPULATING CUSTOMERS TO SPEND MORE

In the world of academia, the Chartered Institute of Marketing (CIM) defines marketing as the management process responsible for identifying, anticipating, and satisfying customer requirements profitably. CIM also adds that successful marketing depends upon addressing many key issues, including the following: What is a company going to produce? How much is it going to charge? How is it going to deliver its products or services to the customers? How is it going to tell its customers about its products and services? Traditionally, these considerations were known as the four Ps, but as marketing has become a very sophisticated discipline, a fifth P was added —People—and recently, the six and seven ones—Process and Physical evidence.

Many businesses have equated marketing with neurolinguistics programming and many market tricks. The tools are many, but unraveling the puzzle is quite simple. Manipulation is not merely the absence of good communication; rather, it grows out of specific misconceptions and communication dysfunctions. Once you develop the ability to detect manipulation, you will dramatically improve your effectiveness at judging and discovering companies that use manipulation. To identify manipulation in any business regardless of the size and the industry, look for one or more of its major hallmarks through answering the following questions:

- Does the business make money out of satisfying people's real needs or desires?
- Does the business create meaningful products and services that genuinely benefit and empower people?
- Is the business a problem solver or a problem creator?
- What is the source of the profits?

The answers to these questions determine whether a company is using manipulation to sway their customers into buying their products and using their services. If you doubt the answers to these questions for any company, then it exists to make a profit only and profits are the center of their universe, not your needs. Furthermore, the work environment in such companies tends to be unfulfilling for their people, as their jobs are meaningless. Meaning in one's job comes from doing something for the greater good; thus, contributing to the fulfillment of other people. Such businesses tend to produce products that are unneeded and a prototype of others. They confuse people to choose whatever perfectly suits them.

WE CARE ABOUT YOU, TRUST US. YOU ARE THE CENTER OF THE UNIVERSE.

> Facebook was not created to be a company. It was built to accomplish a social mission—to make the world more open and connected. We think it's essential that everyone who invests in Facebook understands what this mission means to us, how we make decisions and why we do the things we do. At Facebook, we're inspired by technologies that have revolutionized how people spread and consume information. We often talk about inventions like the printing press and the television—by just making communication more efficient, they led to a complete transformation of many important parts of society.

The quote above is an excerpt from the letter that Mark Zuckerberg wrote to investors when Facebook went public. It outlined the company's social mission and its goals for the future. Below are the main ideas that Zuckerberg detailed in his letter about the overall scope of Facebook:

- "Facebook was not created to be a company. It was built to accomplish a social mission–to make the world more open and connected."
- "At Facebook, we're inspired by technologies that have revolutionized how people spread and consume information."

- "Facebook is about the relationship between two people. Relationships are how we discover new ideas, understand our world and ultimately derive long-term happiness."
- The world's economy is screwed because the banks have been playing with real cash like it was a game of Monopoly. But don't worry, as Facebook is here to save the day. "We hope to improve how people connect to businesses and the economy. As people share more, they have access to more opinions from the people they trust about the products and services they use. This makes it easier to discover the best products and improve the quality and efficiency of their lives."
- "Simply put we don't build services to make money; we make money to build better services," wrote Zuckerberg. "And we think this is a good way to create something. These days I think more people want to use services from companies that believe in something beyond simply maximizing profits."
- "We're going public for our employees and our investors. We made a commitment to them when we gave them equity that we'd work hard to make it worth a lot and make it liquid. This IPO is fulfilling our commitment."
- Stop tweaking your privacy settings people—let the world see what you are up to. Come on; this is the reason you tell all about your meaningless life on Facebook, isn't it? Well, even if you are not going to open, Zuckerberg wants Facebook to be as open as possible.

THE REALITY

Facebook was not created to be a company or to accomplish a social mission using technology; it was set up to manipulate the masses' psychology. The social comparison has negatively affected people's behavior when comparing their lives to other people. Who are the best travelers? Who got the most expensive and luxurious cars? Who are the happiest couples? Face-to-face communication has become rare. 'The unsocial media' like Facebook and other platforms have dehumanized the social aspect of people's lives. In fact, they are far from being social. Facebook is the primary driver for feelings of depression, frustration, loneliness, jealousy, and envy.

In the age of Facebookism, Instagramism, and Twitterism, people have been manipulated for so long to behave foolishly. People have become less sociable and isolated. Short tempers and 'I need it done now' are the outcomes of the unsocial media business. Most of the people have become psychologically ill and prisoners within the walls of other people's lives. Facebook was set up as a data-mining project to collect as much information on as many people as they could.

The purpose of this data-mining project that became Facebook was to find out a significant number of things about a significant number of people. Where are they going? What are they doing? What airline are they using? Whom do they associate with? What types of books or movies have they read? Facebook is using manipulation to make use of people's personal information, destroy relationships, and create a society of short-tempered and selfish individuals. But most importantly, they have created a spy tool to be used on all of us. Manipulation has become a business and a profession nowadays. Whether online, face-to-face, or on Facebook, it continues to be the master trade in a globalized world.

MANIPULATING EMPLOYEES TO INCREASE THEIR PRODUCTIVITY

Central to forging any company is the creation of the performance review system that measures and evaluates staff performance. Most companies around the world incentivize and motivate their employees with financial incentives, or 'carrots'. This in turn motivates employees to obtain more carrots, creating a never-ending cycle.

- **CARROTS/MONEY:**

Ivan Pavlov was a Russian physiologist who worked on conditioned responses. He discovered by experimenting on dogs that they learned to associate different stimuli and objects with food. In particular, Pavlov monitored and measured the connections between the dogs, food, and salivary behaviors. Pavlov added a bell to the experiment to use as a stimulus. After providing the dog with food after ringing the bell on several attempts, he rang the bell and saliva secreted from the mouth of the dog even when the food was not provided. Pavlov called this process a conditioned response; the dog associated the food with the bell.

Pay in companies is perceived as a delicious carrot; money motivates the areas in the brain to trigger electrical signals into other regions of the brain. Those signals are enough to create an addiction to the money stimuli. Thus, the person will get addicted to money. Like alcohol, gambling and money addictions are hard to quit. They also affect the primary functions of the brain that are responsible for planning, feeling, and movement. All companies use financial incentives to reward their employees. They manipulate people's brains to release the hormones that sustain the addiction and prolong it.

In the case of Lehman Brothers, the CEO ignored very critical and vital signals about the dangerous situation for his bank. He did not listen because he was not willing to, but because his brain was not functioning properly due to the full activation of the reward circuit. Similar, in the case of Enron, CEO Jeffery Skilling was another prominent victim of money addiction. The over-activation of his brain reward circuit led him to over-leverage the company debt. Like all addicts, they had insatiable greed that made their companies' cultures addictive and toxic as well.

Money is a wonderful manipulator. Corporate leaders have made it worse by making money the only motivator for people. In normal doses, money is good for meeting and sustaining our needs, but when it is the goal, it becomes like alcohol: the more you drink, the more you need it. A fair amount of drink is good but excessive drink makes anyone an addict and quitting is so difficult. We will find how greed triggers the reward circuit in the brain to make people addicted to money and perform actions that they have no control over.

GREED:

Greedy, uncaring, selfish, egocentric, reckless, careless, addictive, short-tempered, emotionless, and deceitful are some of the personality traits of most banking executives and corporate CEOs. The last financial crisis in 2008 has shown us some examples where the previous traits were fully demonstrated. All resulted from money addiction and the extraordinary power that both disrupt the brain's reward system if overstimulated.

THE BRAIN REWARD CIRCUIT:

The more, the better is the primary stimulator of the brain reward circuit. Desires and wants are what stimulate the neural pathways and structures. The longer and the more pleasurable the stimuli are, the stronger the association with the rewards. Money acts on the brain reward system. Overstimulation for a longer period develops desires that are difficult to satisfy since most corporate rewards are designed to fire the neural transmitters and excessively stimulate people's brains to demand more. The challenge for those who design corporate cultures and reward systems today is how to design rewards and compensations systems that nurture people's potential rather than making them greedy.

- **STICKS/FEAR:**

As proposed by Abraham Maslow in the hierarchy of needs, feeling safe is the most basic need that most humans need. It is essential for people to acquire lower needs to move up in the hierarchy and fulfill another need. It was impossible for the employees in Enron and Lehman Brothers to maintain a sense of job security. Behind closed doors the managers ranked, yanked, and decided the future of the employees by scrolling up and down on a 1 to 5 scale with a click of a mouse in front of a big screen in a windowless meeting room. The result was a huge distrust for management. Why commit to a company if people are unsure if they will stay to the next quarter?

MOST EXECUTIVES AND CEOS ARE FEAR MONGERS.

Downsizings, redundancies, performance appraisals, and layoffs are the leading causes of fear in organizations. Most managers influence and control their people's behavior with fear. They are accused of causing massive and real health problems to people across the globe. They are the main contributor to the world's enemy number one: stress. Stress slows learning, interferes with memory, lowers the immune system, and increases blood pressure and heart rates. It kills the human body if people are stressed for longer periods of time. With the over-stressed business environments that have become stress friendly, people's bodies are silently secreting cortisol. The stress hormone almost pumped continuously out in people's bodies has a harmful effect on health. With that in mind, those who motivate their staff with the sticks have facilitated the 'silent killer'. This term is not my invention but is a medical term that refers to untreated hypertension. Corporately speaking, the silent killers are the bad managers and leaders who have become the most critical contributor to stress and anxiety.

COOKING THE BOOKS TO MEET STRINGENT GROWTH TARGETS

The reason the planets orbit the sun is because the gravitational power of the sun keeps them in orbit. The same goes for the moon; the gravity of the earth pulls the moon to revolve in its orbit. The current capitalist system pulls companies to rotate around it. The capitalist system gravitational components are profit as the number one goal, followed by producing unneeded products, manipulating people's desires, and crunching more and giving back less. Do we blame companies because they are cooking their books to meet the unrealistic financial targets to please the analysts and investors expectations? Or should we blame the system?

Companies cook their books in response to the system that is orchestrated and designed by the greedy and selfish egocentric people who are sitting in their unreachable ivory towers. Bending the rules to the desires and pressures of the stock markets has been the practice. It is about posting astronomical earnings and pleasing analysts. Auditors often overlook accounting practices to sell their services and make clients happy instead of detecting potential problems. The obsessive greed of most companies leads them to project earnings that are consistent with the wishes of the investors, analysts, and banks.

Enron, Lehman Brothers, and other corporations and investment banks made their finance departments bend accounting rules to meet high financial expectations. They tried to duplicate their success by hiding the problems and hoping that everything would get better. They had mounting losses and skyrocketing debt in cronies of balance sheets and records. On the surface, their financial statements looked healthy, but they were maliciously cooked to confuse and trick anyone who read them. The unjustified, unstrained growth and greed left fraud unstoppable. Extracting more wealth and exercising greater power justified all the means to achieve the greedy end.

THE SEEDS OF COLLAPSE HAVE BLOSSOMED

"MISTRUST"

In 1990, the Argentinian government launched the digitalization project to modernize the national ID cards for its citizens. It was an open-tender invitation to the national and international companies to implement the project. The sought-after lucrative deal led the German multinational conglomerate Siemens to bribe the Argentinian officials with $70 million to secure it. However, a surprise occurred when a new Argentinian president came into office and implemented major governmental transformations. First of these was to scuttle the deal with Siemens. For Siemens, losing the deal would equal throwing $70 million into the sea. To revive the deal, a second bribe was paid. The bribe was made public and brought unforgettable shame to the company, leading to a significant distrust of the company's dealings internationally.

If we get back to the statement, understanding the roots of the problems changes the response, the scandal contributing factor to Siemens downfall was an aggressive growth strategy that compelled managers to see bribes as a shortcut to hit ambitious performance and financial targets. Greed and power justified all the means to Siemens to unlawfully do what it took to increase their profits by using their power to manipulate the Argentinian officials. It cost Siemens approximately €2 billion to restore confidence in the company. The scandal brought humiliation to not only Siemens' employees but also the whole German nation.

...

In 1998, the Hewlett-Packard Company (HP), an American multinational information technology company, made a parachute jump from its position in the top 10 companies to work for as featured in *Fortune Magazine*. Three years later, HP disappeared entirely off the list. What happened to HP? Competitiveness was favored over innovation and layoffs became an option instead of employees' retention. HP was no longer the lighthouse for the entrepreneurial culture.

When a vase falls over and breaks on the ground into pieces, fixing it is possible, but the cracks are still there. Trust is the same when mistrust occurs; it could be partially restored to a certain level, but not entirely. When the winds of competitiveness swept over HP in 1999 after the new CEO, Carly Fiorina, came into office, distrust among employees grew deeper. Camaraderie, creativity, and job satisfaction were replaced with dissatisfaction and distrust. Layoffs superseded retention and pay raises and bonuses were suspended. Employees distrusted management.

In 1999, Carly Fiorina who was a former candidate for president of the United States in the 2016 election came to replace the retiring chair, Lewis Platt. Carly favored competitiveness over innovation and entrepreneurship. Reinventing HP was her first proposal, which implied reinvigorating the competitive spirit and focusing on speed.

Camaraderie was no longer a priority in the competitive market. The autonomy and creativity that characterized HP business units were replaced with centralization and competitiveness. The entrepreneurial spirit faded away. Pay raises and bonuses were suspended and layoffs came to the fore. The values of disrespect, dissatisfaction, and unfairness were communicated to employees by the new management that led them to increasingly distrust the company. That was the turning point for HP.

If a farm experiences poor crop yields for many seasons, it means three things: the quality of the seeds may be bad, the environment is not suitable for farming, or the farmer crops' cultivation is not proper. Similarly, if a business has been in a state of continuous decline, it means three things: the foundation of the company is shaky, the environment is not fertile for productivity and innovation, or the leaders do not look after their people and show compassion for them.

Trust is the denominator that brings people together to make something happen. Trust emerges out of the values shared by people who work and live in the same environment. Trust is not an organizational structure or training program that management asks people to learn; it is a human feeling that comes out of a natural ability driven by the same beliefs that are upheld by people. Companies that exist to make money do not develop trust among their people, as their communication is manipulative and their environments are discouraging. Their motivation scares and the rewards are unfair.

When trust is low, time is wasted with people second-guessing, doubting, and investigating each other to stay safe. They double-check and micromanage everything. A building becomes vulnerable to collapse as soon as the seeds of mistrust blossom. They grow to develop the first cracks that contribute to the downfall.

THE COLLAPSE IS IRREVERSIBLE

"NON-COOPERATION"

One of the most startling features of our human race is our ability to form groupings, tribes, and societies in which people develop an affinity and attachment to each other. History shows us that cooperating humans had an edge over non-cooperating ones. Strongly bonded groups that share a common destiny survive, as their pursuit bonds the group, eases their differences, and unifies their actions. History also shows us that greed and the power of greed led to the collapse of mighty civilizations and empires. Just as corporations and companies that exist to enrich themselves are doomed. When the whole system comes crashing down, money will not save the boat but rather the strength of the rowers' arms.

When people work for these corporations, they do so not because they love their jobs; they join in the pursuit of paycheck, not happiness. Their loyalty is given to the paycheck, not to the company; it is a game of people for themselves. People get together when a belief unites them, not by a promise of extra dollars in the next salary. When danger threatened money-worshiping companies like Enron and Lehman Brothers, people lamented and cried for the loss of their jobs and not for the downfall of their companies. Such companies had horizontal and vertical cracks that split their companies apart. Edward Smith, the captain of the Titanic, sank with the ship, whereas the captains of Enron and Lehman Brothers sank the ship and rescued themselves.

Companies that make money an empowering vision and believe joy is in its pursuit turn their people into selfish individuals who are willing to do whatever it takes to generate more money regardless of their actions toward others. Competition, greed, and selfishness govern people's behavior; therefore, playing the cooperative game and assuming a social responsibility would be impossible. All their sights are fixated on making the numbers. "If anyone tells you that there is a single-factor explanation for societal collapse," says collapse guru Jared Diamond, "you know right away that he or she is an idiot. This is a complicated subject. There is always a conflict between the short-term interests of the elites and the long-term interests of the whole society. Those at the top extract more and their selfish interests always outpace their people."

AN ACCIDENT IS NOT A COINCIDENCE; IT IS A SERIES OF INCIDENTS

The idea of the collapse pyramid (Figure 1) is a thorough observation of history to learn for the future. *H. sapiens* progressed to reach a key milestone in human history by adopting a sharing culture that changed later to an accumulating one. A series of ups and downs characterized the human journey. History shows us profound examples that any failure that happened in the past is most likely to occur in the future and, conversely, any success that happened in the past is expected to be repeated in the future. My role here is not only to shed light on past events but also to provide a paradigm that can be used as a learning tool to correct the path and stop history from repeating itself. An accident is not a coincidence; it is a series of incidents connected in a pattern with a foundation that is the main contributor to its fall.

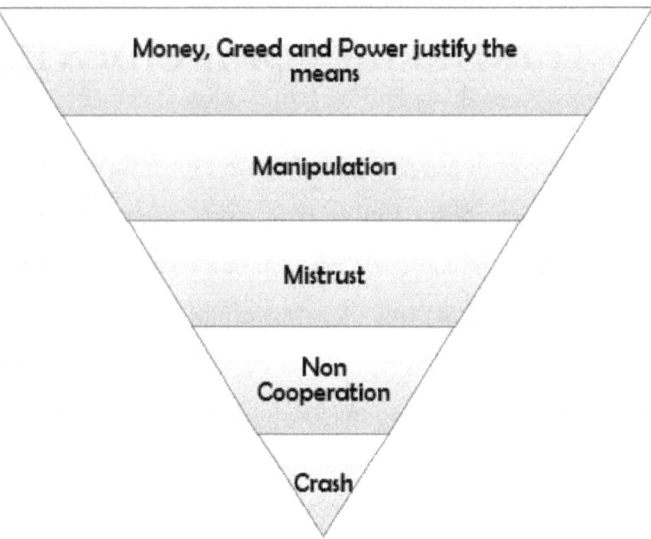

Figure 1: The Collapse Pyramid

The critical insight driving this chapter is the hard lessons of history. The collapse pyramid does more than sum the problems that led to the major collapses throughout history. It provides an approach to overcoming them. However, the greater challenge is the degree to which we can understand the downs of the past to achieve a powerful problem-solving effect in the future. The reason the pyramid is inverted is to highlight the analogy between its foundation and the downfall. Greed, manipulation, conflicts of interests, unethical behaviors, loss of transparency, exploitation, cheating, authoritarian rule, corruption, instability, fragile values, and fighting over resources are the outcomes of its foundation. Looking at things from a different perspective, we can observe that those at the top have always felt "greed and power justify all the means."

Considering an accurate diagnosis of the problems in the collapse pyramid, leaders who are aware of them have the chance to correct them through hard work and coordinated action. Correction involves diagnosing the problems to solve them. The avoidance of the hard work of correcting a specific failure will lead to another one in the future. It is unstoppable. Enron's collapse has been an excellent lesson for all to learn. But has its collapse forced the thoughts of business leaders to retain a powerful appeal to critical thinking and learning?

After all, executives, consultants, and business gurus have spent years of education, observation, and experience learning about the causes. The collapse pyramid works by shedding light on the crucial factors and provides a pathway to substantially understand the nature of its trajectory. Enron's collapse shocked the world and raised hundreds of questions about its demise. The biggest challenge for leaders is to understand what happened and how to avoid its recurrence in the future.

COMPANIES DO NOT FALL OVER BY THEMSELVES; LEADERS PUSH THEM TO THE EDGE

A significant amount of time has been spent thinking and talking about the past. Trends have been drawn to connect the dots to predict the future. Connecting the dots to provide a clear insight is what we hope to persist far in the future. What might happen to humanity in this century or beyond? The collapse pyramid has given us some clues about the past. Will that permit us to form new thinking about the future?

The future is unpredictable. Some events are indeed unpredictable because sudden, unexpected, and external changes cause them. Some events are predictable because they are our own making and we have absolute control over them. The best we can do is develop an internal immunity system for the things that are under our control to face the challenges that are sudden and out of our control. The world economy will remain volatile, the competitors will keep competing, and everything around us will constantly change.

The declining trajectory has continued its momentum despite short corrections. We have a big responsibility to stand firm and reverse the declining trajectory of history that threatens the near and long future of our humanity. Our capabilities are enormous, and the future is in our hands right now. What we need only is an action that unites all of us, and then even the most powerful declines will be faded by our combined strength.

CHAPTER FIVE

TOWARDS A UNIVERSALLY ACCEPTED DEFINITION AND STANDARD FOR LEADERSHIP

Most rulers throughout history clung to influential positions to preserve their wealth. They made their great civilizations and empires destined to fail then fall because of their greed and insatiable appetite for acquiring more and giving back less. Today, corporations are merely wealth extractors; they claim they are advancing the interests of the society through their businesses while their companies cause more suffering to individuals, society, and the environment.

Most companies produce products that appeal to our desires but not our real needs. Luring people into buying stuff they do not need is the theology of consumerism. Producers strive to constantly manipulate people to drive them away from connecting with things that are worthwhile. The pursuit of profits has made companies mistreat their employees and resort to layoffs to balance the books.

It is time to undertake a major reformation of the current standing system of corporate capitalism, especially given its countless adverse consequences at the business, social, and environmental levels. Capitalism has become an evil in undermining and decimating human ideals by negatively impacting people's lives. Crony capitalism has promoted poor management practices which have accelerated the dehumanization in the business world. Immediate intervention is deemed necessary to reverse the dehumanization. The only way to do this is to redefine entrepreneurship and leadership by focusing on their real meanings and understanding their actions.

REDEFINING ENTREPRENEURSHIP ABOUT ITS TRUE MEANING:

THE HIERARCHY OF BUSINESS NEEDS

The core concept of the hierarchy of human needs (HHN) proposed by Abraham Maslow, an American psychologist, in 1943 is that no one can be fulfilled unless other essential needs have been met. Maslow invented the hierarchy of needs to describe the paradigm through which human needs move through. He divided the human needs into deficiency needs and growth needs. The attainment of the self-actualization at the top of the human needs relies on satisfying and achieving the lower needs like feeling safe and having a sense of belonging and self-esteem.

Humans have both lower and higher needs and they must fulfill the lower needs to reach the higher ones. Businesses are no different; they must have their basic lower needs met before reaching the higher ones. This begs the question: What are the lower and the higher needs of any business regardless of the size and the industry?

The foundation of a great business is the reflection of its leader or founder's purpose. This is simply the challenge the leader sets to solve in a business model. Businesses do not have purposes, their leaders do. A company is just a group of people. Great businesses are measured by their leaders' purposes in terms of their clarity and consistency. It is the leader's purpose that draws the big picture for the whole business, its broader contribution, and its final impact.

In principle, great businesses should be purpose driven and should be established on the mark of contributing to the real needs of people. It is about starting or restarting a business that solves a problem and creates value for the whole society and not only for the owners and the shareholders. It is the pursuit of the businesses to contribute beyond making money and short-term interests. Great businesses are born entrepreneurially when their leaders' sights are always fixated on finding solutions to the problems facing people. It is also about satisfying customers' true needs, not desires. It is about making jobs more meaningful for the employees. In purpose-driven companies, business owners come up with great ideas and turn them into products and services that benefit people.

The failure of most businesses stems from their inability to determine why they exist. What are they trying to achieve? Most businesses talk about their competitive advantages or unique selling points, but what they call a competitive advantage is vague and can hardly be understood. Essentially, a competitive advantage is how they gain superiority over rivals using pricing, features, marketing, and different attributes. Being competitive means you are focused on being the best. It is a narrow scope that leads nowhere. Talking about purpose and meeting people's real needs excludes us from using the term competitive advantage, as it implies and encourages a process that serves no other purpose but to trick people. Many companies have destroyed their businesses out of securing and protecting their competitive advantages even though they were unsure of what set them apart from the crowd. Ultimately, profit maximization is the number one goal and decisions are always expressed in financial terms.

WHAT IS THE ALTERNATIVE?

Does an entrepreneur desire to make money or an impact? Answering this question determines the source of inspiration for the entrepreneur. The key difference between a good and a bad business is how people easily identify the business purpose, which is the purpose of the entrepreneur. Most entrepreneurs' bottom line is how they make money, which is undoubtedly essential for any business. People do not live to eat; they eat to live. What is the grand purpose? Successful and great entrepreneurs focus on the impact they want to make and make money out of enhancing this positive impact for people.

Leading companies do not compete; they lead. They strive to do great things. Leading companies do not have competitive advantages, they have leading ones. Finding a true leading advantage is how business leaders demonstrate entrepreneurship and leadership in action, not in words. What is your leading advantage that is not related to competitiveness? This is the right question to ask since it sums up the purpose of the business and its core values.

Discovering and determining your leading advantage will become the spark that fuels inspiration and propels people into action. Inspiration and leadership are symbiotically linked. Inspiration becomes infertile and turns into manipulation when businesses exist to compete rather than lead. Why does the business exist? What is its purpose?

- What is the challenge that the business is set to overcome for all?
- What are the positive contributions that the business brings to the whole society?
- What is the overall impact on people's lives?

Having a purpose is not only good to have, it is a *must* have. Purpose is a source of power. It is how companies communicate their values and leverage their impact. Most companies say that they have all the tools, resources, and sources to create a competitive advantage. You can have all the tools and the resources to build the ship, but setting your destination is more important. Embarking on discovering your leading edge requires you to discover your purpose first.

Leadership should not be blindly pursued; it should be first understood. Understanding why you are in business in the first place and the impact that you set to create is crucial. It is about setting the destination before pulling the resources to build the ship. It is about discovering the purpose of the business before embarking on the journey.

If the business cause or purpose is clear, it will be a magnet for the people who share the same destiny. If the business is solving a problem facing people, it educates as it raises awareness about the problem and the solution.

Most people admire great leaders because they truly inspire them. Such inspiration comes from the fact they stand for something great and sacrifice their time and energy in their pursuit to achieve that great cause. It is through focusing on the cause that the business advocates for the solutions to human problems, satisfying true needs and not desires, and making jobs more meaningful. This inspires people to work hard to advance what the business stands for because they want to achieve it for themselves as well.

The mass manipulation that the business undertakes in its communication and operation with the public comes at a cost. Distrusting the business. Essentially, people trust businesses that meet their true needs and not confuse them based on trivial differences in products' attributes. Me-too companies and products are a manifestation of bad competition that only serves to confuse and trick people. On the other hand, businesses which are driven by a purpose beyond profit stimulate good competition which is the key to continuous development.

The final impact created by the business is the main determinant of the soundness, relevance, and genuineness of its purpose. The final impact is of utmost importance and tops all the other needs in the hierarchy. I call it the hierarchy of business needs (HBN). These needs constitute a sound approach into sound entrepreneurship, which paves the way to forming the approach into sound capitalism. The HBN enables people to use a common moral sense to discern businesses that make a positive impact from those that do not. It is a higher kind of capitalism. It is capitalism as it was ultimately meant to be: meeting essential needs, not competing for differences. It is about finding those opportunities that will unleash the greatest possibility of addressing these social problems.

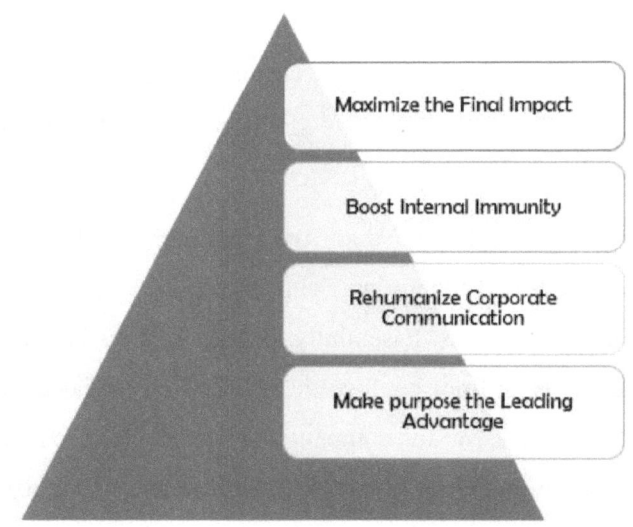

FIGURE 2: THE HIERARCHY OF BUSINESS NEEDS (HBN)

The HBN addresses the overall impact of the business from how it inspires and fulfills employees' needs to how it adds and creates value for customers. Companies that understand and conceive the HBN as their foundation improve other businesses. They do so by inspiring and positively encouraging others to learn and improve their offerings. It fosters good competition. The HBN enables companies to lead and contribute to the well-being and the fulfillment of people. Thus, they thrive and unquestionably last.

REDEFINING LEADERSHIP ABOUT ITS TRUE MEANING:

THE HIERARCHY OF HUMAN NEEDS

In today's global economy financial crises, seizures, panics, and meltdowns are the master scene. The absence of leadership has made redundancies, layoffs, downsizing, resizing, and restructuring the norm in the business world. The responsibility to change this situation has become huge, and it hinges on the leaders' shoulders. The problem in most companies and organizations around the world is that they miss and overlook the key physiological and psychological elements that shape and influence people's behavior, social inclusion, productivity, and motivation.

The failure of companies to engage and retain their people is because they are unable to look after their basic human needs. Therefore, it is through the hierarchy of needs, known as Maslow's hierarchy of needs, leaders must understand that permanent and stable jobs are the minimum basic needs for all employees. Encouraging autonomy and fostering people's sense of belonging to the group in which their efforts and contributions are recognized, valued, and celebrated are so vital. People cannot be fulfilled unless they positively touch other people's lives, as this constitutes the core of self-actualization and self-transcendence in the hierarchy of needs.

Managers and leaders in all businesses around the world have a human responsibility towards their people. They should ensure that their employees' lower and higher needs are met and cared for before talking about retention and engagement. Talking about employees' retention and engagement wastes time if layoffs and redundancies are business practices. You cannot expect people to be productive when your crucial task as a manager or a leader is to scare them. Feeling safe and secure is one of the most critical needs. It is about survival. When people feel threatened, unsafe, or unstable, they will ultimately fail to play the cooperative game.

The HHN is a significant step and a great tool in the hands of leaders for encouraging employees to achieve themselves first and celebrate their achievements before contributing to others (i.e., the customers). Making the HHN the foundation of the business is the hallmark of inspiring and humane leadership. Companies create true value if they care genuinely for the fulfillment of other people. Great leaders are the ones who can build and apply the HHN on a scale at which leadership capacity is evaluated. The number of people inside the organization who are working towards their fullest potential is the primary determinant of great leadership.

To tap into the deep satisfaction and the fulfillment of the customers, companies need to refocus their emphasis on their employees. Who is in charge of the customer's fulfillment? Certainly, it is not the CEO and the executive management team who deal with the customers; it is the employees. If the employees are not fulfilled, they cannot channel their fulfillment to customers through the products they make and the services they deliver. If employees are uninspired by the purpose of their business, ensuring the customer's fulfillment does not happen.

Most businesses pay less attention to the higher needs of their employees and customers. Fulfilling employees and customers' higher needs demands time and quality that subsequently reduce profit margins. Therefore, most companies produce for people's lower needs because they require fewer resources. However, companies that care for the fulfillment of their employees create value for their customers. Businesses that are willing to create innovative and creative products want an atmosphere for their employees in which innovation and creativity are harnessed and welcomed. Growing and deepening the employees' fulfillment leads to the same for the customer. It is always reciprocal.

Both the hierarchies of business and human needs present a thoughtfully innovative, empowering, and, most importantly, great business culture. These concepts are two sides of a balanced equation. The delicate dance between both hierarchies is called "entrepreneurial leadership." They harness the power of self-interest for the good of society. They also form the determining factor for separating the businesses that produce for real human needs from those that do not and this helps to understand the major distinction between leaders and non-leaders.

1ST, THE HIERARCHY OF BUSINESS NEEDS (HBN)

REDEFINING ENTREPRENEURSHIP ABOUT ITS TRUE MEANING

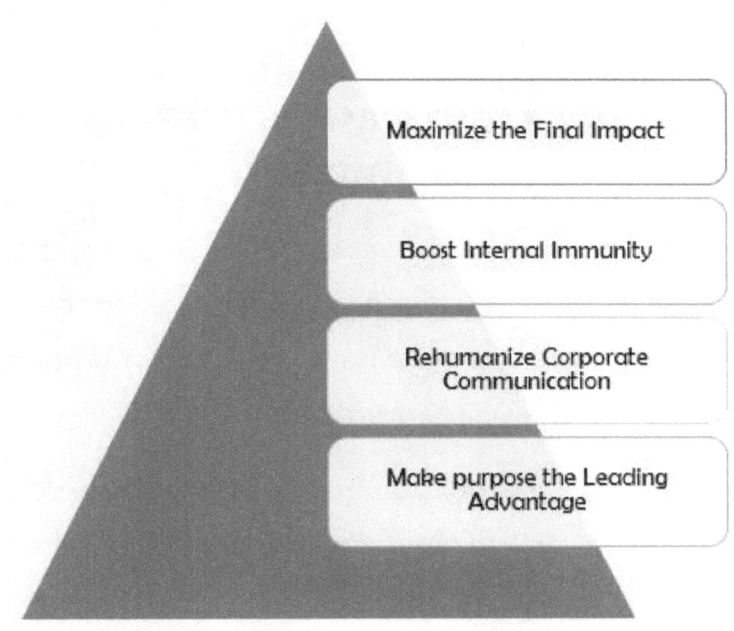

FIGURE 2: THE HIERARCHY OF BUSINESS NEEDS (HBN)

...

TWO KINDS OF COMPANIES OPERATE IN THE WORLD.

The first seeks to maximize the positive impacts for people through solving the problems facing them. The other maximizes profits by ignoring or creating problems.

The first one is genuinely empowering people, and the other one is negatively impacting them.

PURPOSE IS THE LEADING ADVANTAGE

Most companies' CEOs, executives, and managers spend long hours behind closed doors to steer and advance the ship. Many complicated graphs, presentations, and a thick pile of papers are employed to invent the competitive advantage that will make them different and unique. They want to unravel the secret recipe that will transform their business to be a market leader. They use competitor, market and SWOT analyses, six sigma, balanced scorecards, PESTs, and many complicated financial models to try and stay ahead of their competitors. They are looking for the competitive advantage that guarantees a defeat for their enemies, namely their competitors.

The problem is that business owners missed the most important single factor that gave birth to the company when they discuss its survival and thriving strategy. It is the purpose of the business and the cause of its existence. A purpose is born when the company is created. The problem arises when entrepreneurs who built the company forget to form its purpose. Most companies look for a market opportunity and pour money into seizing their share. This is how most companies start. Money is the purpose. As the company begins to decline financially, they resort to their complicated charts and graphs to adjust and stay afloat. As they struggle to identify what caused the sudden decline, they engage in relentless attempts to explain the causes and suggest remedies.

Delivering excellent customer service at affordable and competitive prices is not the reason behind creating a business. Transforming the lives of customers is an outcome achieved in undergoing the business. Also, changing the world to be a better place is clueless. Nurturing the human potential does not capture the essence of the challenge. Leading the industry with innovative products does not tell us why you are leading the industry. Also, using a colorful language does not make the statements more appealing.

Acceptance comes from understanding the challenge that led to the birth of the company. Most women go into labor before delivering their babies. The same is for creating and delivering a purpose. It is always hard work. It requires the leaders to describe the challenge that they are going through. If the challenge is unidentifiable from every single angle, there is a malformed purpose.

Leadership matters when leaders articulate the purpose to identify the challenge, solve it, create value for all, educate people, leverage the impact, inspire change, and nurture needs. Creating a purpose that does not include all of that is just an abstract statement that serves no purpose at all. We will see in the next section that communicating purpose and making it the leading advantage will communicate the contributions and the final impact of the business. The leading advantage does not occur automatically; it requires leaders to embed it in all communication and critical functions of the business, including marketing, HR, operations, decision-making, and strategic planning. The purpose is the oxygen of the whole organization, not a piece of paper hung on the wall.

WHAT MAKES A GREAT PURPOSE IN BUSINESS?

A great purpose in business reflects the leader's purpose. If the leader's purpose is unidentifiable, then the business purpose does not exist at all. If the leader is purposeless, the business offerings are purposeless. It is a balanced equation. Companies do not have a purpose, their leaders do. Thus, the greatness of the business purpose is determined by the clarity of the leader's purpose in terms of its meaning and impact.

Attempting to gauge the soundness of a business purpose requires discovering the soundness of the leader's purpose. But how do you determine if a purpose is genuinely born and not artificially manufactured or adopted? The most reliable way is to ask questions and assess whether the final impact on people's lives is positive or negative.

McDonald's, the American fast food company and one of the largest fast food restaurant chains in the world, claims it exists to provide its customers with food of a high standard, quick service, and value for money. We could use the following questions to examine the soundness of their purpose and its positive impact.

1. Why does the business exist?
2. What is the business trying to achieve, solve, and challenge?
3. Does the business make money out of satisfying people's desire or true needs?
4. Is the business a problem solver or a problem creator?
5. What is the source of the profits?
6. What is the final impact on people's lives, society, and the whole world?
7. Does the business create meaningful products and services that genuinely benefit and empower people?
8. Does the business have a safe, empowering, and happy environment for the employees?
9. Does the business use layoffs and redundancies to balance its books?
10. Do you feel that you are a valued human being when using their products and services or just a paying customer?

The importance of these questions is that they will enable people to identify good businesses from the bad. Ultimately, two kinds of companies operate in the world. The first seeks to maximize the positive impacts for people through solving the problems facing them. The other maximizes profits by ignoring or creating problems. The first one is genuinely empowering people, and the other one is negatively impacting them. You can judge for yourself whether McDonald's final impact is a positive or a negative one.

...

They exist to make and maximize profits. Their methodology is based on assessing the material possessions of people. Their business model hinges on sinking people into more debt and enslaving them to serve the debt all their lives. "Tell me how much you have, and I will tell you how much I will give you." Delaying a mortgage payment will risk the repossession of your house. Penalties and litigations against people who are late in repaying their loans are the most common courses of action.

Grameen Bank, a microfinance bank in Bangladesh, changed the rules with the belief that credit should be accepted as a human right and that people who do not possess anything should get the highest priority in getting a loan. Muhammad Yunus, the economist who pioneered the concept of microfinance, derived the name of his bank from the Bangladeshi word for village. He believed in helping the poor to unleash their potential. He started his bank to uplift the impoverished people of his country by empowering them to improve their working and living conditions. Grameen Bank has taken many initiatives to help people get out of poverty. The bank extended credit to the unemployed, the poor, the illiterate, and different classes of people. Muhammad Yunus believes that even the poorest people have the potential to develop and build their lives. He established his bank based on the following principles:

- Poverty is not a condition that poor people are born with. It is created and stimulated by the institutions that are unwilling to support a specific segment of people.
- Credit gives people the means to experiment and to take initiatives. It will lift them out of poverty and pay off their debt.
- Charitable donations are not a cure for poverty. They prolong it. They make people dependent and stifle the spirit of initiative to combat poverty. Empowering people and nurturing their potential is the answer to poverty.

Grameen Bank not only facilitated extending microcredit to people to start their projects but also tackled the most important question, "Why are people poor?" Yunus constantly strived to provide solutions to the recurrent problem of poverty, and subsequently, Grameen Bank has focused on assessing and unleashing people's potential rather than evaluating the amount of collateral they have. This is the main difference between an entrepreneurial venture that drives prosperity for all and a business that exists only to make money.

...

"End human suffering in the world as it relates to technology" is the mission of Menlo Innovations, a Michigan-based company in the United States.

According to their website, "Beyond the joy of delivering high-quality software to our clients, the most gratifying part of our work is the stories of the impact that our software and process has on our clients, users, and our team. We call this The Menlo Effect." Menlo has gained an international reputation because of its purposeful and joyful culture, which was deliberately designed and built by its founder, Richard Sheridan.

End human suffering in the world as it relates to technology is their daily business, and their mission is an action statement that inspires everyone who works at Menlo to show up every day fully determined to turn the IT industry upside down. Richard Sheridan has pumped fear out of the room. There are no hierarchies at Menlo. The organizational approach at Menlo is horizontal, meaning there are no layers of managers or barriers. Exchanging feedback is flexible and informal, often conducted over lunches, during stand-up meetings, and casually around the table. A safe working environment triggers trust. It encourages collaboration and creativity. Everyone has the opportunity to ask questions and receive feedback. They have a truly humane working environment.

Menlo's culture is cultivated by a great purpose and constantly looked after by a purposeful leader. It is their brand. "At Menlo, we do more than design and build great software. Not that great software is a small thing. It's rare. But we aim for something higher. Our processes, our culture, our work ethic—they all aim toward a single goal: joy". It is their way. It's all about JOY.

...

Companies like Menlo Innovations and Grameen Bank are shining examples of businesses that solve a problem while making money. They see themselves as advocates of prosperity, not profitability. Addressing many of the world's most challenging problems is how they continuously strive to deliver long-term economic and social values with sustainable and global solutions. This can only be achieved by standing firm for what they believe in and inspiring others to join them. Such companies aspire to do more than just run businesses. They want to inspire building a better world, and their success is defined by how many people show up to follow their lead and be part of their missions.

LEADERSHIP DEMANDS A NEW WAY OF COMMUNICATION:

REHUMANIZING CORPORATE COMMUNICATION

As a leader, you cannot build and inspire others if all the laws of leadership are violated. Yielding significant impacts requires a thorough understanding of what great leadership is. As far as great leadership is concerned, there is no grey area. There are only great leaders who inspire and care for people. Others who do not fall under this category are not leaders, and there is nothing wrong with that. The importance of this reiteration is that great leadership cannot be reached unless a revolutionized way of communication is adopted and promoted.

"Leaders should not only revolutionize their communication but rehumanize it." Using the current method of corporate communication is a great victory for crony capitalism, which has taken over every aspect of people's lives. The crony capitalist system demonstrates that humans are not yet at the center and emphasis is still on the pace of production and the exponential growth of profits. Great leadership demands a new way of communication that is revolutionized and rehumanized.

Leaders speak proudly about corporate achievements but their actions rarely reflect significant changes in people's lives. This makes it difficult to discern which companies are worth praising and how many leaders deserve our respect and attention. Most corporate cultures have discouraged leaders from making any serious attempts to carry out a major transformation. One of the most common failures for most leaders is that they are overtaken by a mechanical and corporate communication that only serves to demotivate and stress people.

In answer to all the challenges, one sound and a simple idea is to rehumanize the corporate way of communication. Leaders have a significant responsibility to inspire a humane way of communication. To do that, leaders must agree on a new system that must eradicate the old one. The new system should start with rehumanizing the dehumanized way of communication.

HOW TO REHUMANIZE CORPORATE COMMUNICATION AND TURN IT INTO INSPIRATION

COMMUNICATE YOUR PURPOSE AS YOUR LEADING ADVANTAGE.

Many companies around the world deploy and employ different tactics and strategies to promote and sell their services, both traditionally and digitally. Steve Jobs once said that marketing is about values. It is about creating value, learning, and practicing how to communicate and add value to people. This is the core of good business and meaningful marketing. Creating and producing useful stuff that adds real value to people is far more important than creating the noise they call marketing. Indeed, huge amounts of time, energy, and money are spent daily to create unneeded products and services that people are reluctant to buy. Communicating a true leading advantage is the solution, as it helps the business to fly over the noise. It fosters the positive impact that the business creates; in other words, how the world will change and improve by using your products and services.

Communicating your leading advantage means talking about the difference you are trying to make. What is the challenge you are trying to solve? What are the positive contributions you are trying to deliver? If you have a clear, purposeful, and meaningful leading advantage, people will create a rapport with you. They will be aligned with the way you are trying to uplift and fulfill them. The purpose of good communication is to let your customers identify and explore the full range of benefits you are providing to them. This type of communication is derived from the purpose of the business and its leading advantage.

REDEFINE AND REHUMANIZE CORPORATE JARGON.

The mechanical and factory language that has prevailed since the 17th and 18th centuries has made it not only necessary but also compulsory for leaders to revolutionize and rehumanize communication. Communication is the oxygen of a great culture, and leaders who underestimate the power of using humane communication will risk losing their title of leader. Touching the lives of people positively is a critical component of great communication and is a tremendous motivational power. Communicating a meaningful purpose implies making a difference in people's lives.

Unfortunately, poor corporate communication has adversely affected people by devaluing and diminishing the true sense of people as human beings. Some of the most dehumanizing words include employees, customers, consumers, human resources, management, hiring, etc. These words have subconsciously become part of most leaders' mindsets. They should be eliminated. A change does not happen overnight, but the leaders who have the willingness to change can adapt quickly.

The idea of managing and controlling things is logistically and technically understandable, but the notion of managing and controlling people is dehumanizing. People strive to be inspired and empowered, not controlled, monitored, and managed. Managing people in organizations is even a taught MBA course in most business schools and evidently practiced in most companies around the world. Manageable items include assets, capital, machinery, land, stock, systems, but not people. This major difference should be understood and applied.

Therefore, from here onward, I will use words that have humane connotations that add and convey meaning to people. For instance, the word employees will be replaced with associates. According to the dictionary, an employee is someone who works for someone else, whereas an associate is a person who you work with or spend time with, indicating a level of companionship or camaraderie. For instance, if your manager were to tell you that you are a great associate, partner, or employee, which would make you more feel more valuable as a human being?

The dehumanized approach has heavily dominated most businesses' cultures and communication since the 17th and 18th centuries. However, moving to a rehumanized approach cannot be seen as a desire, it is a *must*. Upholding and advancing a cause demand a new way of communication focused on inspiration. What must be understood is that inspiration is not corporately manufactured; rather, it emerges at the birth of the business purpose.

HOW IS INSPIRATION BORN?

I used to turn the radio dial very slowly by hand to search for a station that sounded interesting to me. Most of the time, finding it required me to turn the radio knob to the left and to the right slowly until something piqued my interest. The same happens when you click with something or someone that you love, admire, are inspired by, or socially connected to. When people are inspired, they are emotionally engaged and they devote the mental capacity to solve problems and work out new solutions.

When we are emotionally connected, the neural networks are stimulated by the received communication through our visual and audible organs. Our neural networks, which are a sequence of larger chains of neurons, form neural units through crystallization and stimulation, and these store the way we interpret and envision the world. These neural units are the set of ideologies, beliefs, and memories in our brains.

Knowing this basic biology helps us to understand how inspiration works with regards to companies. Companies are social settings that should be distinguished by their belief systems, communication, and social and professional codes.

KICKING OFF INSPIRATION IN THE BRAIN REQUIRES ZERO ACTIVATION OF THE AMYGDALA

The amygdala is the brain's panic button; it is responsible for the body's fight or flight response. It sets off a chain of biological changes and reactions that prepare the body to respond to the danger. When people agree and share the same beliefs and ideas, the amygdala is almost switched off, harmony kicks in, and a deeper emotional connection is achieved. When neural networks become activated, a stronger stimulation leads to a faster firing and greater mental and emotional engagement. We understand from this neurological mechanism that uncertainty is the enemy of inspiration. *Mental and emotional engagement requires an almost zero activation of the amygdala.*

Companies that use layoffs, redundancies, and harsh performance reviews constantly trigger the amygdala and keep it alerted to prepare the body for the fight or the flight response. As explained, uncertainty causes stress, and more oxygen and glucose are needed by the body. The main parts of the brain are diverted from creative thinking and problem solving. In other words, when a hungry tiger is in sight, there is no room for creativity and one's leg muscles are the only competitive advantage. Kicking off inspiration requires leaders to perfect the constant soothing of the amygdala. Creating a permanent sense of certainty for people impacts the neural dynamic in their brains, whereas uncertainty, which is often caused by job insecurity-related concerns, forces people to only look after their basic needs.

When people are inspired by their leaders, friends, and others, their beliefs are very similar and there is absolute conformity in the way they envision the world. Inspiration is a neurological reaction in the brain. It is not a psychological one. It should be reiterated that the mental and emotional engagement requires an almost zero activation of the amygdala. Making people less susceptible to fear and anxieties inhibits cortisol secretion and floods oxytocin into their brains. Consequently, people feel emotionally rewarded and connected, after which trust emerges and cooperation follows. Undoubtedly, if these people are working together, their level of achievement will be matchless.

The leaders' most and foremost responsibility is to uphold causes, champion them, and then choose the right people who genuinely believe in them. By doing so, the believers would be inspired and work hard to advance the cause.

• • •

Leaders do not lead; they inspire us and those who do also care for us. As such, we trust them, and they trust us to do the next big thing not only for them but for all of us.

BOOSTING INTERNAL IMMUNITY

DEEPENING TRUST AND STRENGTHENING CO-OPERATION AMONG PEOPLE

It is anthropologically and historically known that over the last 100,000 years, humans' instincts were first developed socially then intellectually. As explained in Chapter One of the book, human competencies evolved based on the size of the social circle, interaction, and cooperation among the group. Survival made humans develop instincts such as love, compassion, collaboration, and trust. Throughout history, communication was vital to building organized and massive networks of cooperation among strangers to create communities, empires, and great civilizations. But how did human trust emerge to support such cooperation?

It is essential to understand that if people share the same traditions and beliefs, they naturally and automatically bond together. Religions play a significant part in maintaining order and keeping people together. As soon as humans began to believe in gods and goddesses, they formed groups and cooperated to provide for these beings. Such a belief in a divine and higher authority led people to come together on a massive scale. Moreover, it ensured the social order.

HOW DOES THE BRAIN PROCESS TRUST?

To have a better understanding of how trust emerges, let us define trust in simple terms. Trust in plain English is when you feel safe in the presence of someone else. When we do not feel safe around other people, our brains send the message "Be careful." Trust is triggered neurologically in our brains at two levels:

- The survival level or in the reptilian brain, which controls critical functions such as heart rate and breathing.
- The ideological level or in the limbic brain, which controls our feelings, beliefs, and memories.

For example, when we meet new people the amygdala will send two messages. "Be careful" or "Everything is ok." Fight, flight, or do nothing. This is the first survival mechanism that helps us to interpret the world around us and set the first trust level. The amygdala will then communicate this information to the other regions in the limbic system. These regions will analyze the belief structure in our brains to check if the received communication from the people around us matches. If there is a match, trust will emerge.

Dr. Paul Zak, an American neuroeconomist, discovered that oxytocin is a neurotransmitter that is a major player in the regulation of trust and morality. Thus, it is called the trust hormone. Oxytocin is released in the body when we feel safe and connected; it tells the brain that everything is ok. Dr. Zak determined that the human brain naturally produces oxytocin during breastfeeding, orgasms, hugs, and holding hands. Oxytocin motivates and instigates a variety of social behaviors, including selflessness, compassion, forgiveness, and altruism. The problem is that this hormone cannot be triggered in environments in which fear is the norm.

Imagine you were out shopping for your family. Along the way, you found yourself face to face with an armed gang. In this situation, your brain does not have time to do creative thinking. You will be immediately shifted to a flight or fight response: fighting the gang or escaping them. Sudden and unexpected situations hijack the amygdala. Anyone who has encountered such a case has reported increased heart rate and difficulty breathing, as amygdala activation increases the release of adrenaline hormones.

Although people in the business world will not face ravenous predators or armed gangs, they may feel threatened every day due to the insecurity and uncertainty of their workplaces. The leaders' responsibility is to build environments in which trust is the building block by soothing the amygdala and increasing oxytocin secretion in people's brains. First, businesses should uphold a great cause or purpose, which will attract the likeminded and believers. Inspiration kicks off when people are ideologically, emotionally, and intellectually engaged.

Ensuring jobs are stable will ease the uncertainties and assure the associates that everything is ok. Otherwise, insecurity and instability will prevail. At this point, selfishness emerges and the spiral of decline pushes the whole company to the final crash. This of course happened with Enron, Lehman Brothers, Swissair, and many other money-centric organizations.

COOPERATION REQUIRES A SHARED DESTINY

Have you ever asked yourself why armies are vastly cooperative groups? The same applies to religious groups. Why are gangs so well organized? How did our ancestors cooperate to conquer the world and build the large cities in which we live? Let us answer these questions using our understanding of how trust is triggered. It has been stated previously that trust first developed instinctively as hunters and gatherers approximately 12,000 years ago and then ideologically 2,000 years ago through a shared belief in gods.

Instinctively, humans are social animals, and we use our instincts to identify our enemies and friends. It is the same for animals. It is impossible for deer to trust tigers even though they live together in the same jungle. This instinctive sense plays a critical part in the survival mechanism. Feeling safe is what enables us to trust those around us. But in a world full of complexities and differences, how do we know if we should trust the person who is sitting beside us?

The answer lies in the beliefs and ideologies that people share. Ideological beliefs (i.e., culture) are what reduce conflicts of interests among the same group of individuals. The more you share the others' beliefs, the better you can predict their behavior and the easier it will be for you to decide whether you can trust them to act in your interests in any given situation.

Let's consider the combination of factors that led to the eruptions of most of the Middle East conflicts in what is called the Arab Spring in 2011. In particular, dividing and ruling the region and extracting its wealth by the superpowers come to the fore along with many other factors. Although this constitutes the major contributing factor, deeper systematic roots were exploited to serve a bigger purpose. Ultimately, the goal was to stimulate the sectarian strife. Ignoring this elephant in the room ignores the truth and denies the roots of the problems.

A confrontation with the leading cause is often forgotten. The Middle East countries, especially Syria, are highly sectarian and different faiths and ideologies are being practiced. A war fought between two sides that belong to two different ideological beliefs within the same country has savagely torn the country apart. Trapped in the middle of this war, the Syrian people lost their homes and families. As far as trust and cooperation are concerned in this chapter, it is difficult to redevelop trust among the Syrian people who battled, hated, and continue to fear each other. Strengthening the bond within the Syrian community to end the war is a difficult task. Surviving Syria needs advancing secularism and liberalism that should entirely supersede sectarianism, which people inherited from a long time ago.

As the diversity of our modern cities is increasing the complexity of our lives, people are seeking out new environments of trustworthiness in a culture that suits them best. But most importantly, the culture itself is distinctive; much like a lighthouse that guides those who are looking for it. Human cooperation gained momentum when instinctive and ideological trust was combined with the emergence of religions, beliefs, and natural laws. However, the most compelling question that still determines the level and consistency of cooperation in the future remains unanswered: **Are we genetically cooperative or selfish?**

Answering this question requires us to define natural selection, which is the process through which the most adapted species survive and produce more offspring when faced with fewer resources, a larger number of the group, and harsh weather. Natural selection favors groups that work together and protect each other to live another day. Enrico Goen, the author of *Cells to Civilizations* wrote,

"Consider a unicellular organism; its DNA comprises of long sequences of base pairs strung together forming chromosomes. A mutual incentive exists for nearby bases to cooperate because their close connection means they are likely to be intertwined together. By incentive to cooperate, he does not mean that one base is thinking about the other, but rather what is beneficial to one in terms of reproductive success is also likely to be helpful to the other. In such a situation, natural selection favors outcomes in which nearby bases effectively work together to ensure reproductive success".

As Richard Dawkins, the author of *The Selfish Gene,* explained:

> An organism is a cooperative of genes united by their expectation of a shared route to the future, via eggs or sperms. Life forms are organized as cooperative units, the significance

of a change in one component can only be judged by considering how it interacts with the others. A single letter from a word carries a little meaning in isolation. Hydrogen and oxygen can combine to form molecules of water. Water molecules can come together to form ice. [1]

Richard Dawkins concluded that we should restrain our biological drive and build a more cooperative world. The question is how? Primeval individuals knew that the acceptance of the group was important to survival. Since survival could not be reached individually, selfish infighting was avoided for the greater good of the group.

It must not be forgotten that although a high standard of morality gives a slight or no advantage to everyone and his children over the other men of the same tribe. A tribe including many members who are always ready to aid one another and to sacrifice themselves for the common good will be victorious over most other tribes. When the group shares the same destiny, members of the group cooperate rather than compete to survive. Their tendency to survive reduces their selfish infighting.

---

[1] Dawkins, Richard. (1976, 1989, 2006). *The Selfish Gene*. Oxford University Press.

During the war in 2013 in Syria, two small villages were attacked by militants in the area. The people in the first village were secular, whereas the villagers in the second village were Christian devoted. In the first village, the fighters swept over the first village in two hours due to the fact the villagers were not united to defend the village. The people of the second village were Christian devoted believers upholding a holy mission to protect their church from the ensuing war and from the danger of being desecrated by the militants in case of an attack. Since the villagers in the second village were united around a common cause, their cooperation led to their survival, as they were able to deter the attack of the militants and live another day. That day, the lack of coordination among the locals in the first village led to their inability to defend themselves and their village. They were unable to survive.

When "mine" becomes "ours," everyone will benefit. We can achieve ourselves and we can extend our hands to help others. We can accomplish the self and, at the same time, be selfless. A positive impact is always determined by the degree of selflessness and our collaborative consumption. The power of the sharing community helps us to accomplish difficult things very quickly when others come to our aid. It helps us to make quantum leaps forward instead of smaller steps on our own.

HEALTHY COMPETITION DRIVES LEARNING AND INSPIRES INNOVATION

When Google introduced Gmail and YouTube, they knew that their data storage system was not adequate. They had to figure out what to do about this situation. The head of the infrastructure group at that time was a man named Bill Coughran. Bill allowed two teams to work differently, one team to build on the current system and the other team to build from scratch. Bill's role was to spark the debate between the two teams.

When Build It from Scratch team shared their prototype with the group. Their design had many limitations. As the need for a solution became more urgent, it became clear that the existing solution was the right one for the moment. So, they selected that one.

The whole process took nearly two years. Early in that process, one of the engineers had gone to Bill and said, "We are all too busy for this inefficient system of running parallel experiments. But as the process unfolded, he began to understand the wisdom of allowing talented people to play out their passions. He admitted, "If you had forced us to all be on one team, we might have focused on proving who was right and winning and not on learning and discovering what was the best answer for Google".

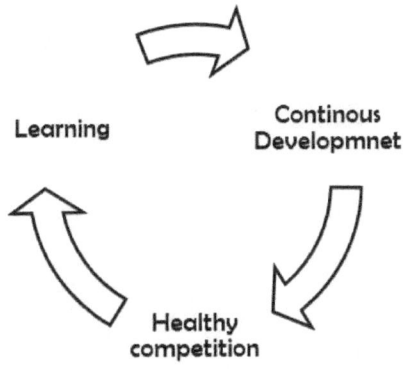

Figure 3: Competition Positive Feedback Loop

ADAM SMITH AND KARL MARX

Contrary to Karl Marx, a Prussian-born philosopher and economist who believed in revolutions to restore justice to the masses, Adam Smith, a Scottish economist and philosopher, valued order and stability. Selfishness, greed, and inequality are the outcomes of capitalism as proposed by Karl Marx. They lead to injustice and instability in society. In contrast, Smith considered the capitalist system the ideal economic system.

Marx criticized capitalist institutions as far away from being the natural components of a functioning society. Marx's view was that the working class was being exploited by the capitalists for selfish gains. In the battle between capitalism and communism, capitalism won and continued to be the governing force that controls the market regardless of the adverse consequences. However, without Smith's ideologies, Marx would not have been able to define his theory in relation to Smith's notion of capitalism. It was this continual contrast and competition that spurred a continual path for further improvement.

In business, good competition is galvanized by the higher callings that companies exist for. Learning from others is the key to continuous progress. The accumulation and the sharing of ideas, experiences, concepts, arts, and science are what enabled humans to build such great civilizations and cultures throughout history to our modern day. The purposeful companies observe and learn from others to improve their offerings, not to stay ahead of their competitors. Companies that are highly focused on their journey and what they are trying to achieve learn and advance their business. Learning is far more important than competing. The most powerful system that enabled humans to reach greater heights is learning and sharing. The power of good competition is learning, and the beauty of learning is continuous improvement that serves everyone.

Discovering the flaws of competitors does not add up to improving the quality of the products: it intensifies the competition and stifles innovation. Nevertheless, innovation does require a degree of good competition to instigate learning and foster cooperation. Good competition challenges companies to defeat problems and handle hardships facing people. It does not mean facing the opponents on a battlefield. Healthy competition pushes companies into discovering new things, not to outpace others and declare a win. Outsmarting others is a manifestation of bad competition. Adopting the mindset of a healthy competition requires leaders whose purpose guides their mindset and determines their outcomes. Accordingly, their sights must be fixated on what their business is trying to solve and contribute.

...

The power of good competition is learning, and the beauty of learning is continuous improvement.

BAD COMPETITION DRIVES GREED AND LEADS TO BAD OUTCOMES

The unethical behavior of leaders can be compared to an avalanche. The amount of snow in an avalanche varies based on many factors, but it always has the potential to bury a whole valley under dozens of feet of snow. Similarly, unethical behavior of leaders occurs when a conflux of bad acts catalyzes a critical incident or triggers an event that pushes everything to the edge of the mountain, similar to an avalanche. Just as an avalanche may result in damaging loss of property, personal injury, and death, unethical leadership behavior ruins all involved, including leaders, people, organizations, and the whole society.

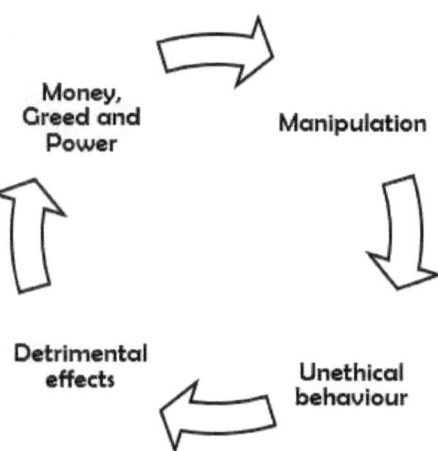

Figure 4: Competition Negative Feedback Loop

Unethical behavior, which is driven by greed, insulates people from the consequences of their actions. "When the pursuit of self-interest runs unchecked, it leads to socially fatal outcomes. Volkswagen (VW), a German car company, has damaged its industry and other large corporations by hiding the amount of pollution that some of its diesel engines emit. Such behavior provoked fresh doubts about whether large corporations could be trusted to act honestly and ethically. The scandal is significant not only because VW is one of the world's largest vehicle makers trusted by consumers for its technology and reliability, but because cars can kill. When a company hides a lethal flaw, as General Motors did in the United States with faulty ignition switches and VW did with diesel engines that produce nitrogen oxide emissions, it has a deadly toll. In response, VW has set aside €6 million to compensate consumers and pay fines and they have pledged rapid reform.

Other companies have been accused of altering laboratory tests in a way that exaggerated real-world results. For instance, some automakers competed fiercely to obtain laboratory certificates promising that their cars were fuel-efficient. Bad competition evokes scandals where rules are twisted and regulations bent to gain a competitive advantage. This often occurs in highly regulated sectors, such as financial services, and ultimately destroys an industry's image and leads to a fierce regulatory backlash.

THE FINAL IMPACT OF THE BUSINESS DETERMINES THE SOUNDNESS OF ITS PURPOSE

Developing and implementing the HBN is the central task of leaders. It provides a solid foundation and an insight into the way of cultivating people's efforts to obtain robust results and create innovative solutions. It is a coherent and inspiring structure that yields results that respond to high-stakes challenges in a globalized economy. Adopting a sound entrepreneurial approach by using the HBN drives great business value for all. However, with innovation as a goal for most businesses, determination can also turn into frustration since working towards being innovative is amorphous. An excellent way to avoid such frustration and foster innovation is to understand the final impact that you are trying to accomplish. Innovation is not a purpose that thrives on its own.

Innovation is an outcome that was well interpreted and applied by Menlo Innovations, which pioneered new rules for innovation. Richard Sheridan built a company whose purpose is to challenge the status quo in relation to the information technology industry. His ultimate goal is to end people's suffering using technology. They exist to fulfil this mission. This is the final impact that they want to create. As mentioned previously, he built the culture inside Menlo to support this purpose. Joy, enthusiasm, flexibility, making mistakes, no fear, and working in pairs are the building blocks of this culture. Richard Sheridan created a belief system and culture that have lifted the company up to incredible creativity and innovation in what they do and deliver.

It is impossible to put people in a room and instruct them to innovate and be creative. Innovation is not a bullet point on a job description; it is a series of actions and interactions among people in a specific environment. It does not happen instantaneously. Innovation requires many correlated factors to ensure its occurrence. It always needs specific catalysts.

Innovation happens in an environment where people are inspired to yearn for solutions together, think freely without boundaries, and feel safe to give and share their different ideas. It cannot be done unless people feel safe, belong to the environment in which they achieve their self-esteem, and believe they are part of what they produce and deliver to the whole world. This is what gives people a sense of fulfillment, status, and pride. No one can be creative without first feeling safe. Those who do not feel safe are not worried about being fulfilled; they are concerned with whether they will have a job tomorrow.

A CULTURE OF INNOVATION IS NOT SIMPLY DEFINED, IMPLEMENTED,

AND THEN LEFT ON ITS OWN TO SUCCEED OR FAIL.

Menlo Innovations is an inspiring and useful case that can be used to describe how companies live up to their genuine responsibility to society. This is how Mr. Sheridan built Menlo. He understood how to accomplish the mission of building a purposeful and a humane business that nurtures people's potential to create innovative solutions and end human suffering in the world as it relates to technology.

REDEFINING LEADERSHIP TO REDEFINE CAPITALISM

The "ism" of capitalism is to make money out of money. The capitalism dogma is to invest, produce, sell, make a profit, and maximize it. By investing and selling products, the owners of the business will enjoy the financial rewards and provide the products that people need. This is the core philosophy of the 18th century philosopher Adam Smith, known as the father of modern economics.

Over the last 200 years, a divergence occurred between capitalism as envisioned by Adam Smith and today's capitalism. Economists, investors, academics, and entrepreneurs have attempted to explain capitalism versus other ideologies, such as communism. Most hold the optimistic view that capitalism encourages free enterprise that boosts economic productivity, whereas systems like communism have failed to do so since they are hugely centralized and involuntary.

Free enterprise and capitalism are used together to express the view that capitalist goods are produced and sold to buyers at given prices and purchased voluntarily by the people. The supply and demand regulate the market and determine the economic value, and this became the cornerstone of the argument favoring capitalism over other ideologies. Making money out of money and maximizing profits irrespective of the quality of the products and the working conditions for people have characterized the capitalist narrative. Capitalism intuitively implies capital in terms of its preservation and maximization. It refers to wealth creation and accumulation.

Unfortunately, capitalism does not distinguish between good and bad business.

A crucial difference exists between the amount of value created by companies and the amount of money they generate. Capitalism can hardly be measured and understood regarding creating value but can be quickly judged by looking at the monetary values or the profit indices. Capitalism is understood as the accumulation of money: the more, the better. So how do we merge value and profit into *good* capitalism?

The most sought-after reformation for capitalism currently is how policymakers manage it as a regulated market system that incentivizes businesses to contribute to the real needs of people. The hierarchies of business and human needs can be used as metrics to distinguish the real contributors from non-contributors, or those who strive to solve a problem in a business model from those who profit from creating a problem through the business. For instance, Bill Gates made billions through Microsoft, but he also created value through many products that solved problems for companies all over the world. In contrast, McDonald's is burdening most countries' populations with a list of problems, the least of which is obesity and diabetes, especially for children.

This distinction should be acknowledged and observed. Who are the good and the bad capitalists? The purpose and impact of the business is the answer to this question. Capitalism can be greatly understood and applied correctly if viewed from this angle. Grameen Bank and Menlo Innovations are problem-solving companies that challenge the status quo as well as make money. Understanding the HBN as a system through which businesses respond to high stake challenges and solve problems is a useful framework for assessing purpose. The larger the number of purposeful businesses, the better the world is.

If capitalism is judged by the amount of money created, then the metric is money. If capitalism is judged based on the ability to produce products and services that genuinely benefit people, then the metric is the business purpose and its impact.

. . .
How do business leaders merge purpose and profit into a good business is the hallmark of great entrepreneurship?

REDEFINING LEADERSHIP ABOUT ITS TRUE MEANING

THE HIERARCHY OF HUMAN NEEDS

When Abraham Harold Maslow, an American psychologist, examined the human psyche in 1943, he developed the HHN based on the realization that some needs take precedence over others. He created the five layers of human needs, which are the needs for safety and security, love and belonging, self-esteem, self-actualization, and self-transcendence.

According to the hierarchy, when people have water, food, and a roof over their heads, they naturally seek safety. Once they feel safe, people seek grouping and socialization. At this stage, people tend to achieve themselves and affirm their self-value or worth. If the judgment of oneself is well praised, people move on to find their life purpose and live it. However, only approximately 2% of the world's population ever reaches self-actualization as suggested by Maslow.

While writing this chapter, some people argued with me about whether people can be selfless without being fulfilled. The simple answer is that you cannot give to others while your cup is still empty. No one can flood the world with selflessness and generosity from a drained ocean. The constant altruistic selflessness measures the depth of your fulfillment. In other words, those who experience deeper self-actualization are able to maintain self-transcendence for a longer period.

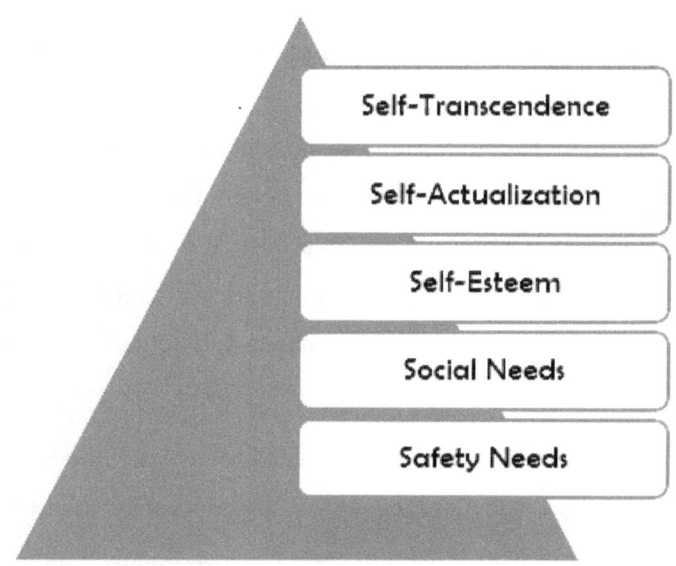

Figure 5: The Hierarchy of Human Needs

THE SAFETY AND SECURITY NEEDS:

When we encounter any situation in the environment around us, the fear region (i.e., the amygdala) detects potential threats and makes sure that we react to it by analyzing the environment. Feeling safe helps us to take care of our other needs.

Corporately speaking, feeling safe and settled in companies like Enron, Lehman Brothers, and many money-centric companies was unattainable in light of the daily greedy, selfish, and stressful environments that threatened the jobs of the people. The language of intimidation that prevailed in these companies was enough to continually hijack the amygdala of all associates. This meant they were on high alert all the time, and that shut down neurologically all the key brain functions. All their basic and lower needs were unmet. They lacked focus and were worried about losing their jobs. The fight or flight response was their governing response.

The case is different for people who are working in purpose-driven companies that put their people first. This focus creates a true sense of belonging inside the organization where people treat each other like a family. Even though people are still subconsciously monitoring what is going on through their amygdala, it becomes less active and negative emotions diminish when they are in a safe environment with happy faces. In other words, people drop their shields. Leadership becomes great when leaders provide supportive environments that are conducive to greater cooperation.

THE SOCIAL AND BELONGING NEEDS:

It is neurologically proven that when people are lonely and feel isolated, the area of the brain responsible for pain shows extra activity and vibration. Associates who feel isolated and socially disengaged in the workplace suffer neurologically, which affects them psychologically and physically. Subsequently, they will be reluctant to give to their company because the company or the environment stands in their way.

Fruitful collaboration depends on social relationships. Once people feel safe and make a stronger social connection with each other, fear and stress go away and people start to trust each other. In his book, Joy, Inc. How We Built a Workplace People Love, Richard Sheridan wrote, "When we pump fear out of the room and give the team permission to make mistakes, the team starts to feel safe. If team members feel safe, they trust one another and if they trust one another, they will begin to collaborate, and we see teamwork".

Maslow's hierarchy of needs emphasizes the importance of fulfilling lower needs before reaching, the higher ones. You cannot be happy and joyful if you are threatened with the possibility of losing your job or rumored news about a redundancy plan. Having and enjoying a sense of belonging will pave the way to fulfilling other needs, including self-esteem needs.

SELF-ESTEEM:

Self-esteem refers to a person's overall evaluation of their own worth. Poor self-esteem can lead people to become depressed. In great companies, leaders create social environments that reward people at the level of recognizing their achievement and celebrating their success. People become more confident, and this drives their sense of accomplishment. If the lower needs of people are met, their self-esteem tends to grow and develop. Money-centric organizations that pit people against one another to motivate them indirectly tell them that there will be winners and losers and that destroys the sense of cooperation.

It is almost impossible to tap into self-actualization for people who work in money-driven organizations, as their contribution to the fulfillment of others does not exist because money is the only motivator. Since fulfillment is driven by the contribution to the well-being of others, their jobs do not serve this purpose, they are meaningless and do not instigate a deeper satisfaction. The blame hinges on the shoulders of the owners and the CEOs whose concern is to enrich themselves and please the shareholders. By doing so, they disregard the highest level in the hierarchy, which is self-actualization.

SELF-ACTUALIZATION:

Self-actualized is reached by those who have found their life purpose and created meaning for their lives. Maslow proposed that 2% of the world's population has reached self-actualization and achieved incredible experiences and results. The self-actualized enjoy deeper personal relationships with fewer friends and family members; their social circles are small and do not involve shallow relationships. In today's business world, making a profit is the number one goal, and therefore most companies and corporations have failed because of the selfish and the greedy behavior of their leaders and managers.

Surrounding themselves with like-minded people, those at the top adopted the language of selfishness as the foundation of their business philosophy. If organizations are self-centered and money-centric, their business environments are discouraging for their associates and unconducive for their growth. In such environments, it is impossible for people to communicate and cooperate, as they are worried about the security of their jobs. Fear, stress, and anxiety prevail and that negatively affects the well-being of people and hinders their productivity.

Purposeful organizations deliberately exist to make a difference in people's lives. They are part of a mission that is bigger than themselves. They want to contribute to the world beyond the walls of their companies. People show up every day to be part of the purpose. Contrary to the money-centric organizations, the jobs will be meaningful, communication will be positive, and cooperation will be natural. As a result, people can climb the hierarchy of needs, as the environment is safe, supportive, and growth inducing.

SELF-TRANSCENDENCE:

Maslow described self-transcendence as those who have reached fulfillment through living a meaningful and purposeful life. People cannot transcend themselves and add to other people's fulfilment if they are unfulfilled themselves. This is the main difference between the levels of self-actualization and self-transcendence: people must self-actualize first before extending themselves to serve others. Self-transcendence cannot precede self-actualization. Albert Einstein agreed when he said, "The true value of a human being is determined primarily by the measure and the sense in which he has attained liberation from the self."

In the business world, the self-transcended leader is the person who transcends the organizational boundary and focuses on the whole society. The self-transcended leader views the financial outcomes and the goals of the production as the means to achieve a higher end. Self-transcended leaders are fully aware that their organizations can have an impact not only within their organizations but socially, environmentally, economically, and globally. It is the ultimate and the most profound description of what a great leader is.

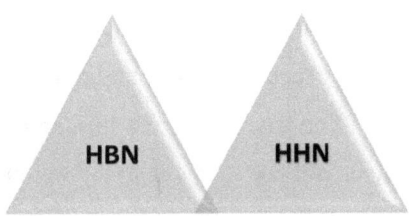

Building a great business requires fostering the synergy between the hierarchies of business and human needs.

CHAPTER SIX

THE POWER OF QUESTIONS IS POWERFUL

5 Ws AND AN H

Analyzing the rise and fall of civilizations has given us a great insight into the causes and the consequences of these occurrences. Since we reviewed the roots of the problems, the main challenge is to identify them, provide the mechanisms to solve them and stop the declining trajectory. Businesses have lost sight of people as human beings in the pursuit of money. Bad capitalism has made businesses produce unneeded products and deliver unneeded services. These products are made solely for increasing profit margins, regardless of the quality.

Profits have become the means and the end. Most corporations and companies have discounted human value deliberately and converted people increasingly into tradable commodities that are bought, sold, and disposed of. That, in turn, affected people's lives negatively and brought dire consequences to our humanity. The whole world has been inflicted.

What is the solution?

Why is it important?

How do we do it?

Who can do it?

Where to start?

When do we start?

WHAT IS THE SOLUTION?

Understanding and implementing the hierarchies of business and human needs can help to identify the potential areas into building leading businesses that lead the big reformation.

WHY ARE THE HIERARCHIES OF BUSINESS AND HUMAN NEEDS SO IMPORTANT?

The financial aspect of all businesses is to stay in business, grow, and make profits. No one can claim the prophetic status in business as if they are the missionaries of love and peace. The key difference is that none of us exists in this life as humans to eat. Food is essential for our survival, but it is not the purpose of our existence. Understanding this point paves the way into understanding leadership and the concept of having a purpose. Arguing this point is baseless and reflects the narrow-mindedness of the proponents. For leaders, the following discussion is of paramount importance.

The absence of a clear definition for leadership and a standard of measurement have confused everyone. When people talk about entirely different things, they experience different views, which lead to different terms and implications. The outcomes will also be different. The interpretability of leadership has confused people as it means different things to different people. Quantifying the qualities and traits that distinguish leaders do not work towards a standard that is unanimously agreed among people.

Although passion, courage, enthusiasm, and integrity as well as an ability to communicate and delegate are must haves, they do not make great leaders on their own. Also, different leadership styles such as strategic, transformational, cross-cultural, facilitative, servant, democratic, situational, and charismatic and many other styles can be confusing. The confusion comes from the difficulty in choosing the best style that is suitable for a particular circumstance.

A mark or standard upon which the leaders' contributions are measured and easily judged is needed. The measurement should look beyond making money and short-term interests. Establishing a universally agreed upon standard enables people and all organizations to understand what they are working towards and aspiring to accomplish. The definiteness of the definition and the standard limit the ambiguity and clear the confusion. As such, the importance of the hierarchies of business and human needs is that they do not only redefine leadership about its true meaning, they provide the scale to discern the contributors from the non-contributors and the leaders from the non-leaders.

Below are the main objectives of the hierarchies of business and human needs. Their power is crucial to help leaders leverage the impact of their businesses through the following:

1. Discovering and harnessing the power of their purpose, the leading advantage.

2. Responding to high-stakes challenges and solving big problems facing people.

3. Meeting the true and the higher needs of people not their desires.

4. Creating purposeful and meaningful products, not just goods with trivial differences in shapes and colors.

5. Educating people about the best options for them and letting them choose.

6. Redefining and rehumanizing corporate communication.

7. Attracting the right people to the organization and revolutionizing the recruitment process to make purpose and values the metrics, not the skills.

8. Creating safe, social, joyful, and growth-inducing environments for people inside businesses.

9. Empowering associates to unleash their potential to tap into the fulfilment of their customers.

10. Delivering superior and unbeatable financial performance to owners, shareholders, and investors.

11. Building a stable business.

12. Providing simple, practical, and memorable metrics that allow people to separate the good from the bad businesses.

13. Providing a general framework for understanding the principles of a sound business.

14. Laying the groundwork for applying the rules of capitalism as a sound system, not a deliberate destructive system.

As twins are siblings carried together in the womb and born at the same time, both hierarchies are twins and complementary to each other. The function of the DNA is similar; each strand has its key function to ensure the transmission of the genetic information for the development and function of the living things. It is the same with regards to the hierarchies of business and human needs. The first one is mainly concerned with creating purposeful products that genuinely benefit people. The second one is about creating a caring environment that helps associates fulfill their potential to tap into their customers' fulfillment.

The hierarchies of business and human needs are very important to building leading companies. Leading companies considerably lead on how they contribute positively. These companies inherently know that creating value for all enhances their leading position. They build and maximize their purpose and its impact to maximize their profits. They make money out of solving problems. In this rapidly ever-changing world, the leaders of these businesses understood the equation and played its rules. They learned that immunity is an internal strategy that is to be boosted to work against external infections. Boosting business immunity means fostering the synergy between the purpose of the business and its impact. This is the leading advantage that ensures the stability and profitability of a business.

Since business executives are obsessed with financial performance, their case is that implementing the hierarchies of business and human needs is time-consuming and in turn reduces profit margins. They argue that there is no time for such an investment in a highly competitive world. However, if someone wants to test the strength and sustainability of a business, it is advisable to examine its resilience in times of crisis. After the 9/11 attacks in the United States, most airlines incurred huge losses as the number of passengers dropped and stock prices plummeted. Redundancies and downsizings were the answer for most of the companies to account for the losses and the weak cash flow.

In stark contrast, Southwest Airlines Co., a major US airline headquartered in Dallas, Texas, reported strong financial performance following 9/11. Their secret is revealed in the statement made by CEO Jim Parker on October 8, 2001, "We are willing to suffer some damage, even to our stock price, to protect the jobs of our people."

In times of crises, companies that put people before customers and numbers showed even stronger financial positions. Southwest Airlines is an inverted pyramid organization where the upper management is at the bottom and staff are at the top. The decisions are made by everyone in the organization, not just senior management. They follow the adage that companies do not make the numbers, people do.

HOW CAN BUSINESSES INCORPORATE THE HIERARCHIES OF BUSINESS AND HUMAN NEEDS? WHO CAN INCORPORATE THEM?

Bad design and a weak foundation are the contributing factors to the collapse of any building. In these cases, certainly, the architects and the civil engineers are at fault, not the workers who build the building. Even a well-designed building will not stand on a bad foundation. The engineers' top priority is to ensure the accuracy of the design and its implementation. Likewise, the failure of any business is the leaders' responsibility from the time of establishing the purpose and the vision of the business to reaching the customers. The leaders are responsible for building a strong foundation and creating an environment that is safe and conducive to cooperation.

LEADERS CREATE IDEOLOGIES AND CHAMPION BELIEFS

Adopting an attitude of universal responsibility is necessary. To do this, business leaders must form an ideology, which is a clear indication of what their companies stand for in the world. Ending human suffering as it relates to technology in Menlo Innovations is a great purpose that is ideology driven. All human beings, including the poorest, are endowed with endless potential is also a great purpose and a belief that is deeply rooted in Grameen Bank.

Ideologies are more than traditional and abstract vision statements; they are comprised of a systematic body of beliefs, philosophies, and concepts about human life. Such ideologies inspire and organize the attitudes and other social norms shared by members of the group. A great purpose statement should mirror the impact on people lives regardless of the products they sell. This is called integrity.

The responsibility of organizations is not to write and hang decorated vision statements on their walls, it is to translate them into real actions. Every company, no matter what its philosophical view, should be founded primarily on the purpose of creating value for people. Championing the ideology and putting it forward translates the power of the belief system into ripples of lasting impacts.

inspiration is putting the ideology into action

Nelson Mandela, a symbol of the struggle against apartheid in South Africa has been a source of inspiration (not motivation) for people around the globe. Mandela did not write fluffy statements and announce aspirational slogans about the importance of campaigning against the apartheid; he spent 27 years in jail as a political prisoner for that cause. He was a man of action. This is what I mean by ideology; it is a firm conviction in a cause and the glue that holds people together in good and bad times. It is an action, and the consistency of the action is instrumental. If leaders uphold ideologies and communicate them, people will be able to recognize a match between the expressed ideologies and their own. If people are not aware of what leaders stand for, reasoning and questioning will govern their engagement with the environment.

LEADERS ATTRACT BELIEVERS, NOT SKEPTICS

It is evident that the lessons learned from history are easily forgettable. Throughout history, the same pattern has kept repeating itself, showing people's failure to avoid the recurrence of the same problems. We learned in Chapter Two that the military leaders made grave mistakes that contributed to the downfall of the entire Roman Empire. Specifically, Gaius Marius, one of the military leaders in 107 BC, changed the recruitment process of the soldiers and recruited non-Roman soldiers who were paid to join the Roman army. Consequently, their loyalty was not to the Roman Empire, but to the amounts of money paid to them by the military commanders. The paid soldiers were fighting for money, and they were unwilling to risk their lives.

The sense of patriotism for the Romans deteriorated massively, and they became indifferent to the destiny of their empire. When it comes to bringing the right people to the right organization, the question is, 'Are you are going to recruit Romans or non-Romans for your empire?' In other words, are you going to want people who are loyal to the purpose and the destiny of the organization or those who only work for paychecks? Great leaders attract people who belong to their tribal community, belief system, and culture.

When people share the same ideologies and beliefs as leaders do, they become attracted to the same cause. In South Africa, Nelson Mandela believed that everyone should be treated equally and many South Africans shared that belief. They were all campaigning against apartheid, rallied around the same cause, ideology, and belief. Mandela ignited the spark that inspired those in the dark to reach the destination that they always wished for. The ultimate test of the ideology power is in the way of attracting the believers, not the skeptics. Let us consider this example below of an advertised job opportunity for the position of priest in the Catholic Church to examine how attracting the people who share the same ideology and belief is critical in attracting the right people.

POSITION SUMMARY:

A Roman Catholic priest is needed to coordinate and participate in Roman Catholic religious functions as required. Must adhere to the principles of Roman Catholicism service in guiding behaviors, philosophy, and mission in all aspects of job performance.

Education

Master's degree in an area of the discipline of theology, ordination, and ecclesiastical endorsement.

Experience

Prefer two to three years of pastoral experience after ordination.

These are the requirements that the church needs to get the priest on board. Let us consider the position summary again; the church needs a Roman Catholic priest to coordinate and participate in Roman Catholic religious functions. Assuming some of the applications were from non-Catholic denominations, such as Orthodox or Protestant denominations, would the Catholic Church consider them? No. Although they might possess all the credentials and qualifications to assume the job, they do not follow and believe in the Catholic faith. What matters is the belief, not the credentials.

Why is it different entirely in the business world? The ideologies and the beliefs that drive the purpose of the business should be the determining factors in choosing the right people. Competency matters, but it does not add up to bringing the right people to the right organization. Businesses are not made up of structure and policies; they are made up of people. Choosing the right people who share the same cause ensures the longevity and sustainability of the business. It is the primary success factor with regards to building a great culture.

Attracting the believers, not the skeptics, ensures that those who share the same belief have a firm conviction in the business ideology, and therefore their loyalty is unquestionable and undisputed. Identifying if people believe in a specific ideology or cause hinges on the shoulders of the leaders. The main problem today is that 99% of companies worldwide hire based on skills instead of purpose and values.

Skills and competencies do not matter; every organization needs people who fit the tribe's customs, values, and traditions. It should be known that partnering up with the right people does not happen in a 30-minute interview. All recruiters who proudly say that they can shortlist the right candidates in 6 seconds are ignorant. To attract those who believe in the company ideals, a radical change should be in the hiring 'partnering up' process to make recruitment based on values and beliefs not on a set of technical skills and competencies. Anyone can be taught a skill, but no one can be forced to believe in something.

LEADERS CREATE ENVIRONMENTS THAT GENUINELY EMPOWER PEOPLE

After selecting the right people who believe and belong to the same ideology and belief, it is essential to create an empowering environment to unleash their potential. Richard Sheridan, CEO at Menlo Innovations, understood the hierarchy of needs very well. He realized that his people would not invent the 'big thing' unless they felt safe. He started his company with the goal of creating a workplace in which everyone is working towards the goal of ending human suffering through technology.

As Sheridan stated, "Freedom from fear requires feeling safe. If you feel safe, you run experiments. You stop asking permission. You avoid long, mind-numbing meetings. You create a new kind of culture in which you accept that mistakes and setbacks are inevitable." At Menlo, the culture is constant collaboration to achieve that end. Constant collaboration means continually transferring knowledge to one another. Collaboration is a major driver of well-being because it leads to strong social bonds.

The advantage of a well-designed work environment is that it leads to high levels of thinking and creativity for companies that provide a greater collaboration experience for their people and celebrate their achievements. The result will be people who feel part of the company's mission every day and are most likely to bring their best energy to the office. In other words, they give their all. The secret to

Menlo's culture comes down to Sheridan's leadership. He leverages people's skills and experiences to support those around them. This is what team, innovation, and collaboration are all about.

Great purpose, camaraderie, joy, a sense of belonging, and collaboration inside Menlo inspire and instigate people's fulfillment to tap into their customers' fulfillment. The idea that innovation is not a solo dancer and always needs a partner is a formula that is well understood and finely implemented. It is one of the best shining examples of a purposeful leading business. Many people have argued with me that such companies do not exist. The reality is that Menlo Innovations is a live demonstration of a vibrant, joyful, and leading company. If you want to understand the true meaning of entrepreneurial leadership, I encourage you to visit their website and read more about their inspiring story.

WHERE CAN WE BUILD THE HIERARCHIES OF BUSINESS AND HUMAN NEEDS?

Meeting people's true needs through challenging and solving the world's problems is the responsibility of all, including governments, banks, universities, hospitals, schools, and profit and non-profit organizations. This mission is not confined to certain social business ventures. All should adopt it as a universal formula for building a better business that leads to a better world. Many companies have emerged around the world similar to Menlo Innovations and Southwest Airlines and Grameen Bank. They have assumed a great responsibility in maximizing the solutions facing society today. Notably, this also significantly maximizes their profits, and therefore it is a sound business model. But the responsibility does not hinge on the shoulders of the few leading businesses; rather, it should be the norm in all sectors and industries.

It does not cost money to drive this change, but it does require a radical behavioral change in putting people first before short-term interests. Those who create an environment in which people are the essence sustain their businesses, whereas those who repeat the past mistakes are doomed. Ultimately, a leader's job is merely to inspire people to do great things and look after them while doing so. If you are not that leader, then it is advisable to reconsider your leadership.

START NOW TO ASCEND HIGH, OTHERWISE, THE DOWNFALL IS YOUR DESTINY

If you have a passion, a commitment to making a difference in the world, and an affinity for other fellow humans, then now is the perfect time to start acting on it. The world needs all of us to make the change happen. Adopting the principles of purposeful and humane leadership as an integrated and holistic commitment has set a number of companies apart. We have many global problems, but we lack global and inspiring institutions with leaders who are powerful enough to address them effectively.

Finding a way to solve these and other problems is one of the greatest challenges of our time for leaders. Global problems require global solutions, and they require leaders who can identify them and develop humane solutions to solve them. Changing the world needs a new kind of thinking and new commitments that transcend making a profit. If leaders do not have the vision and the courage to challenge and break the set rules, then change will never occur.

When you work toward any type of social change, hardships must be overcome. You must believe genuinely that what you are doing is right, or else you may become discouraged and give up. There are no ready-made solutions to problems involving social change. Even implementing a purposeful business requires passionate and firm believers, but when you commit yourself to build a better business, you are most likely committing yourself to create a better world.

There is no room for neutrality in campaigning against corporate greed. This is a difficult struggle of uncertain duration but we must act now before it is too late. Leaders who build purposeful and humane businesses will stop the declining trajectory and set their businesses on the thriving path. Those who do not will make the downfall an inevitable destiny and regretting the past will not help as time always runs forwards and never backwards.

LET US REDEFINE LEADERSHIP TO CREATE A BETTER WORLD

Our historical review began with the extinction of the Neanderthals who lived in scattered and small groups 40,000 years ago. These early humans lacked the diversity that characterized modern humans, the *H. sapiens*, whose culture was predicated on the notion that life must be more than just survival. Discovering the world made them work together to pursue their higher calling and survive as a result. Later, farming allowed humans to have a surplus, accumulate wealth, and start trading. However, ultimately, hierarchies were born and greed and power followed until our modern day. These hierarchies of power led civilizations throughout history to fail gradually and then completely fall. This trend has extended its trajectory to bring nations, societies, and companies to their knees.

It is now clear to propose at the end of our analysis in this book that companies follow a declining trajectory when their leaders selfishly enrich themselves at the expense of the whole society. The rate at which companies fall can be affected by the amount of extraction engaged in by their leaders. The selfish short-term interests of the few at the top are a serious matter of concern. In Chapter Four, understanding the roots of the problem has raised our awareness about the fact that greed and power have become irreversible and failures are a constant occurrence. In this money worshipping culture, people have disregarded each other as human beings, and those at the top have seen others as disposable.

In a world in which dehumanization has tightened its grip on people's lives, most companies have become less interested in meeting people's genuine needs. Instead, they have evolved to manufacture desires and sell unneeded products for the sole pursuit of increasing profit margins. They do this primarily by playing on the fears, insecurities, and anxieties of both associates and customers. This dehumanization has made it normal practice for management to ask associates to do more for less under the constant threat of layoffs.

Also, the dehumanization process has seen customers as purchasing machines whose powers are in buying anything that is produced. The religion of consumerism has blinded customers to be more conscious of the ethics of consumption. Consumerism and the pursuit of profits have made companies mistreat their associates and produce products and services that do not meet people's true needs or environmental standards.

In this systematic dehumanization, companies are forced to compromise most of the sound ethical and human values and ideals. It is disgusting to witness and bear all of that. Furthermore, such people and their businesses are continually manipulating the market by claiming entrepreneurial leadership. They have promoted the constant correlation between social status and material advancement that divides people into the 'us vs. them' mentality. It undermines the true community. The true concept of entrepreneurship and leadership is hugely misunderstood, and most people, including leaders, do not know the true meaning.

Most people think that entrepreneurship is about starting, organizing, and managing any enterprise and selling anything to people. They think that leadership is about maintaining that enterprise and managing people. Most Silicon Valley entrepreneurs in the United States want to change the world and make a big impact, but they are mainly concerned with scaling their businesses to be massively profitable.

Entrepreneurship is a serious and genuine attempt at solving big problems that are facing our world. It is about the strong awareness of social and environmental issues and challenges. It is about addressing them in a business model. Entrepreneurship is not about selling shit to people. It is about solving a big problem. It is a big problem for the entire industry. Unfortunately, most entrepreneurs still see money as the ultimate end, which justifies all the means.

For a time, we have held the optimistic view that the world can be changed and become better. But now the world is becoming something different. The dark side has dominated the bright one. Unilateral efforts are praised but are not enough. Change requires a drastic multiplication of the efforts worldwide to make it happen. The challenge in the 21st century is how to overcome the corporate age top-down hierarchies that taught organizations to favor profit maximization and lay people off to balance the books. Dealing with this reality requires leaders who should use and adopt new hierarchies to redefine leadership about its true and humane meaning to reshape the business landscape. In particular, the HBN can be used to harness the power of purpose in business to create real value for people and the HHN can be used to create empowering business environments to nurture associates' potential to tap into the fulfilment of their customers.

Leaders who understand and use the hierarchies of business and human needs as the building blocks of their businesses will be the pioneers of purposeful and humane leadership that creates the momentum to build a better world. Anyone can be a leader if their genuine focus is people. The ignorance and avoidance of the problem can no longer persist. We diagnosed the problem very clearly and identified the solutions. The world requires leaders who are determined to use the purposeful and humane approaches of entrepreneurship and leadership to contribute to a vastly different, humane, and better world in the 21st century.

NOTES

CHAPTER ONE

- Early Modern Homo sapiens, http://anthro.palomar.edu/homo2/mod_homo_4.htm
- Robert Guisepi, The Rise of Civilization In The Middle East And Africa, 1998, http://history-world.org/rise_of_civilization_in_the_midd.htm
- Robin McKie, why did the Neanderthals die out? The guardian, Sunday 2 June 2013, https://www.theguardian.com/science/2013/jun/02/why-did-neanderthals-die-out
- Gary Sanford, Survival of the Fittest: How Homo Sapiens Outlasted Neanderthals to Become Modern-Day Humans , February 25, 2012, https://mic.com/articles/4634/survival-of-the-fittest-how-homo-sapiens-outlasted-neanderthals-to-become-modern-day-humans#.Tq8l8TCIP.
- Author, Yuval Noah Harari, Sapiens: A Brief History of Humankind.
- Authors, Gregory Cochran, Henry Harpending,The 10,000 Year Explosion: How Civilization Accelerated Human Evolution.
- Marco Langbroek, Ice age mentalists: debating neurological and behavioral perspectives on the Neandertal and modern mind, Journal of Anthropological Sciences.
- Joy Hendry, Simon Underdown, Anthropology.
- Chris Stringer, The Origin of Our Species. London, 2011.

CHAPTER TWO

- Yuval Noah Harari, The Agricultural Revolution - Sapiens: A Brief History of humankind.
- History of the world, From Wikipedia, the free encyclopedia.
- The rise of Rome,www.nsms6thgradesocialstudies.weebly.com
- Romulus and Remus, From Wikipedia, the free encyclopedia.

- Peter Heather, The Fall of the Roman Empire, 2005.
- What-Happened-To-The-Ancient-Maya, http://latinamericanhistory.about.com/od/Maya/p/
- Jared Diamond, Collapse: how societies choose to fail or succeed
- Collapse of the Soviet Union 1991, http://www.theblackmosaic.com/collapse-of-the-soviet-union_how/
- Fall of the Soviet Union, http://www.coldwar.org/articles/90s/fall_of_the_soviet_union.asp
- Daron Acemoglu, James A. Robinson, June 2012, 10 Reasons Countries Fall Apart
- Daron Acemoglu, James A. Robinson, Why Nations Fail.

CHAPTER 3

- C. William Thomas, The Rise and Fall of Enron, April 1, 2002
- Bethany McLean, Peter Elkind, The Smartest Guys in the Room: The Amazing Rise and Scandalous Fall of Enron. 26 Nov 2013.
- Reporter: Henry Bonsu, A nation in shock: Swissair crisis.
- Andreas Knorr and Andreas Arndt, Swissair's Collapse –An Economic Analysis. IWIM - Institut für Weltwirtschaft und Internationales Management.
- Fred L. Smith Jr. and Braden Cox, Airline Deregulation UK., http://www.econlib.org/library/Enc/AirlineDeregulation.html
- Stephen Foley, Crash of a titan: The inside story of the fall of Lehman Brothers, http://www.independent.co.uk/news/business/analysis-and-features/crash-of-a-titan-the-inside-story-of-the-fall-of-lehman-brothers-1782714.html.
- Larry McDonald, Patrick Robinson, A Colossal Failure of Common Sense: The Inside Story of the Collapse of Lehman Brothers.

CHAPTER 4

- Finlo Rohrer & Tom de Castella, Mechanical v human: Why do planes crash? BBC News Magazine.
- Lawrence W. Reed, why "Inflation" Is Back, foundation for economic education, Saturday, November 01, 2008.
- The Neolithic Revolution - How Farming Changed the World, ttp://h2g2.com/approved_entry/A2054675
- The purpose of money, http://www.simpletoremember.com/articles/a/the-purpose-of-money/
- The History of Ancient Mesopotamia, http://www.timemaps.com/ancient-mesopotamia-history
- Bourgeoisie, the free dictionary, http://encyclopedia2.thefreedictionary.com/bourgeoisie
- The Real Wealth of Nations: Creating a Caring Economics, Riane Eisler.
- Pope Urban II orders first Crusade, http://www.history.com/this-day-in-history/pope-urban-ii-orders-first-crusade
- Author, Edward L. Bernays, Propaganda.
- Brian Appleyard, The Independent, Shopping around for salvation: The new religion is consumerism and massive malls are its cathedrals. Wednesday 3 November 1993
- Children in cocoa production, From Wikipedia, the free encyclopedia
- The chartered institute of Marketing, CIM,http://www.cim.co.uk/more/getin2marketing/what-is-marketing/
- Author, Simon Sinek, start with WHY.
- Facebook IPO: Letter from Mark Zuckerberg, http://www.telegraph.co.uk/.
- Saul McLeod, Pavlov's Dogs,http://www.simplypsychology.org/
- Christopher Eppig, What Causes Greed? May 16, 2014.
- Ian Robertson, Bankers and the neuroscience of greed, www.theguardian.com.

- Understanding Addiction, http://www.helpguide.org/harvard/how-addiction-hijacks-the-brain.htm
- Hypertension – the 'Silent Killer, http://www.fph.org.uk/uploads/bs_hypertension.pdf
- Zhu Wenzhong & Fu Limin, A Case Study of Siemens' Violation of Business Ethics in Argentine Based On Stakeholder Theory http://journalofbusiness.org/
- Kimberly D. Elsbach, Ileana Stigliani, Amy Stroud, The building of employee distrust: A case study of Hewlett- Packard from 1995-2010.

CHAPTER 5 & 6

- Eric Beinhocker and Nick Hanauer, Redefining capitalism, http://www.mckinsey.com/global-themes/long-term-capitalism/redefining-capitalism
- Maslow's Hierarchy, http://changingminds.org/explanations/needs/maslow.htm
- Carmine Gallo, Steve Jobs: Get Rid of the Crappy Stuff, http://www.forbes.com/
- Southwest Airlines, https://www.southwest.com/html/about-southwest/index.html?tab=5
- Valuing social responsibility programs,http://www.mckinsey.com/business-functions/strategy-and-corporate-finance/our-insights/valuing-social-responsibility-programs
- Ishaan Tharoor, Paving the Way Out of Poverty, www.time.come, Friday, Oct. 13, 2006.
- Alok Jha, where belief is born, www.theguardian.com.
- Mike Wooldridge, Mandela death: How he survived 27 years in prison, http://www.bbc.co.uk/news/world-africa-23618727.

- Maprograms, http://www.mckinsey.com/business-functions/strategy-and-corporate-finance/our-insights/valuing-social-responsibility-programssCivilizations.
- Charles Darwin autobiography (1876).
- Linda A. Hill, Collective Genius: The Art and Practice of Leading Innovation.
- Chris Ciaccia, BlackBerry: Where it all went wrong.
- Adam Alter, how to Build a Collaborative Office Space Like Pixar and Google. http://99u.com/.
- Author, Richard Sheridan, Joy, Inc.: How We Built a Workplace People Love.
- The Hierarchy of Human Needs: Maslow's Model of Motivation, http://personalityspirituality.net/.
- David Rock, Managing with the Brain in Mind, http:/strategy-business.com.
- Self-esteem, from Wikipedia, the free encyclopedia.
- Dr. C. George Boeree, Abraham Maslow, personalities theories.
- Abraham Maslow, http://www.newworldencyclopedia.org/.
- Author Richard Dawkins, The selfish gene.
- Patañjali, www.goodreads.com
- Menlo's Liberty Factory, http://menloinnovations.com/

ACKNOWLEDGEMENTS

Foremost, I would like to dedicate this book to the souls of my parents who taught me manners, wisdom, and ambition. I am eternally grateful to them for their love and sacrifices. To my brother and sister, so thankful to have you back in my life. You have always been a true support for me.

To all my friends who stood by me through all stages of writing this book.

To all the leaders I have had the opportunity to talk to, read their books, and watch: I want to thank you all for being my inspiration.

Finally, I want to thank EVERYONE who ever said anything positive to me or taught me something.

ABOUT THE AUTHOR

At the heart of Kamil's approach is a purpose. He believes that purpose is one of the most powerful tools to make a real positive change in the world. *"Kamil's purpose is to challenge status quos, especially the most dehumanizing to change the way we live our lives."*

Working in various HR roles in different companies spanning the Middle East and the UK and observing the dehumanizing practices exercised by most managers have fuelled Kamil's purpose. Starting in 2015, kamil has put his purpose into action by putting the mistaken business beliefs and poor management practices on spot in his blog kamiltoume.com. His book **Separating Grain from Chaff** is the first head-to-head confrontation with the dehumanizing status quo in the business world.

Kamil helps individuals and organisations to find and harness the power of purpose. You can find out about Kamil's book and other projects by visiting his blog, kamiltoume.com

In his other life, Kamil is a passionate reader, especially in economics. He has developed a passion for debunking the misconceptions about a variety of economic issues. He is also a coffee lover and a chess player. Kamil is a British- Syrian and lives in the UK.

www.ingramcontent.com/pod-product-compliance
Lightning Source LLC
Chambersburg PA
CBHW030632220526
45463CB00004B/1495